Jean Bro

Professor Justin McCornick

Jean Abell

GO
BOAT
CONGO

What It Was Like for One Missionary Family
in the Latter Half of the 20th Century

Go Boat Congo

Copyright © 2019 by Jean Brokaw Abell

All rights reserved.

No part of this book may be used or reproduced in any manner whatsoever without written permission except in the case of brief quotations embodied in critical articles or reviews.

Layout: Marjorie Clark and Jim Abell

Cover design: Rory Clark, Daniel Morgan

Cover photo: The five Abells in 1963, aboard the freighter *African Glade* out of New York bound for Matadi, the port of Congo

Title page photo by Robert Smith

To contact the author, email her at coboatcongo@gmail.com.

Printed in the United States of America

First Edition: December 2019

ISBN: 9781672853859

CONTENTS

To Norman Burt Abell,
my beloved husband for 65 years
and the hero of this book

In the first year of his second term he lost the use of his left arm to polio. After 15 months in the States he returned to Congo for a three-year term, followed by four five-year terms. In 1990, 29 years after he contracted polio, he left Congo for the last time. Behind him were a head nurse's house he built at Sona Bata, a well at Vanga, an improved hospital at Moanza, countless patients he helped with medicine, surgery, prayer, and everywhere he went, nurses or doctors who had absorbed some of his knowledge or wisdom or skill or the spirit that always put the other person's needs first and never gave up.

ACKNOWLEDGEMENTS

First, my amazingly considerate husband, Norman, who encouraged me to write this book and supplied some memories and some valuable letters. If I'd asked him more, there would be more about him in it! As our Portuguese tutor remarked, "Dr. Abell thinks; Mrs. Abell talks."

Then our children. Grace went over the whole book with me, finding every backward apostrophe and extra space, as well as suggesting what could be left out, saved, put in, better expressed.

Jim supplied us with TeamViewer, which made that collaborative effort easy. He also eagerly supplied Word and hours of technical help.

Marjorie and her husband, Rory, encouraged me to self-publish. They know how, so I'm counting on them.

Bob followed in his dad's medical footsteps and shares his commitment to always putting others first. It was Bob who spoke at the dinner where the University of Rochester Medical School gave Norm posthumously their Humanitarian Award.

Then there are the members of my writing club and Peter Muilenburg, a delightful published writer who had the patience to go over every chapter with me. Mary Jean Hirsig also listened to every chapter. Jacquie Beck was the first to say I should write a book. And colleague Marjorie Sharp inspired me by her book.

This memoir is as accurate as my memory will allow, helped a bit by my children. Obviously I don't know the exact words of a conversation between my parents before I was born. In fact, most conversations are not word for word.

A very few names are changed for the sake of privacy.

CHAPTER ONE

On the Way

"I feel dizzy," the young woman standing at the rail remarked.

Her husband laughed gently and explained, "It's the motion of the ship."

Sure enough, the *Queen Elizabeth,* the original vessel of that name, sailing for Europe in 1955, had just left the quiet waters of New York harbor and entered the Atlantic with its swells. With us on deck were Bobby, age three, and Grace, two. Grandma Brokaw had taught Grace to say, "We're going on a boat to Congo."

Actually, when Grace said it, it came out, "Go boat Congo." We had ridden to the pier, taken an elevator to the second story of the building, and thence walked through a covered companionway to the deck—one of the decks of the enormous liner, which seemed like a city, with shops, beauty parlors, and all. We hadn't seen any water. After we'd explored a while, Grace looked up and asked, "Where boat?"

We'd been on the way a long time. I suppose the journey started with our parents. Both Norm's and mine had wanted to become foreign missionaries, as we termed it then. Both had been refused because of the wife's health. Dad Abell finally made it to China with the United Nations Relief and Rehabilitation Administration after World War II, and his family eventually joined him there—except Norm, who was halfway through his senior year of college by then.

My parents never did see China. Mother was devastated. She told me once, "I'd always sung, 'I'll go where you want me to go, dear Lord . . . It may not be on the mountain height or over the stormy sea,' but I was always sure it was to be over the sea."

"Abram," she questioned, "Why? What have they found out about my health that they didn't know before?"

I don't know when Dad got up the courage to tell her, "I wrote to the mission board, saying I thought service on the foreign field would be too hard for you."

And how Mother found the grace to forgive him I will never know, but I know what his feeling was based on.

She must have asked with tears in her voice, "Abram, how could you?"

"Adah, remember that day when we were to meet at 12 o'clock under the clock at Marshall Field?"

"How could I forget?"

"I waited till 12:30 and then started around the store looking for you. There were two clocks."

"And I was waiting for you under the other and couldn't imagine what had become of you."

"You were frantic. Tears were running down your face."

"I thought you must have been run over trying to get there."

"Dearest, if you were that upset a few miles from home, what would it do to you in China if I didn't come home in time and couldn't get word to you?"

2

So they served as home missionaries, and Mother remained a worrywart but survived. When Dad entered the pastorate, each of his churches got not only a fine pastor but also an ideal minister's wife, who could teach at any level, excelled in girls' work, worked with young people, joined the women's society, invited groups to her home, visited in hospital or home with Dad... In a junior high class she discovered that one boy couldn't read. She tutored him every school day until he could. He became teacher of the men's Sunday School class. One year the head of the Baptist girls' organization in New York State was Adah Brokaw, my humble little mother.

Neither couple put pressure on their children to become missionaries, but we came by it naturally. Norm dedicated his life to Christian service at a summer camp during his high school years. I had been impressed with the missionaries who visited our little church, and well before I was ten I had determined to be one too.

We met in college. Norm began his studies aiming for a career in electronics, but various factors changed his mind. His freshman year he took calculus and radio. Radio wasn't a freshman course, and calculus seemed to have nothing to do with math as he had known it. He found both of them difficult. Then religion prof Al Pitcher advised, "If you have skills in technical fields and also in fields that help people, choose helping people. Our society is way ahead in technology and way behind in people relations." Norm remembered that he had taken aptitude tests showing he had abilities needed by a surgeon. Then he got interested in a certain young woman who was determined to be an overseas missionary.

We had met early in our freshman year. Jo, a freshman woman older than the rest of us, was engaged to a man back home, but she encouraged other freshmen to get together. She arranged a double date for her and me. Norm was her date. Now this was wartime. The only men on campus were 17-year-olds, like Norm, and 4-Fs, who had flunked the physical exam for the military. So our president had invited the armed forces to send V-12s, Navy and Marines who attended classes with us. They occupied the freshman women's dorms. And we freshmen women lived in the fraternity houses! Jo brought the men over to my house and introduced them. I looked at Norm and then looked higher and higher and finally reached the top. He measured 6'3". The other fellow, my date, was short with platinum blond hair. Both looked like engineering types, with slide rules dangling from their belts. We took a picnic to the local wayside park, where we sang "Smoke Gets in Your Eyes" and talked about the stars and theology.

After that Norm and I saw each other Sunday evenings at Fireside Fellowship, which happily crowded the pastor's house, but Norm was dating a professor's daughter. About Christmas time they broke up, and in the new semester Norm asked another freshman for a date. She was busy; he tried me. I was not busy, but that first date flopped. For some reason we went to a movie midweek. Norm was working in one of the dining halls, so the film had started before we got there. In those days, freshman women had to be in the dorm by a certain hour; we had to leave before the movie was over. The only time to talk was while hurrying down to the theater or hurrying back to campus.

Fortunately, there was a second date—the first time either of us had ever attended a movie on Sunday. This time we relaxed and talked over a soda, and many dates were to follow.

Summer came; we went to our respective homes in New York State and wrote to each other. Norm's mother invited me to come for a visit, and I did. On the way back to school Norm stopped to visit me. One evening we drove out on Lover's Lane, where Norm asked me to marry him.

"If it's God's will," I replied. It didn't take us long to decide that it was.

Then we had three years to wait. He gave me his fraternity pin at the end of our sophomore year. Instead of singing "Sister Jean has seen the light," my dorm mates exclaimed, "Well, it's about time."

Jean and Norm in the early years

Another year passed before my sweetheart serenade, at the end of which Norm was allowed to come up to my room (!) and put a ring on my finger. We graduated the following May, and in August my dad married us. Norm was accepted at the University of Rochester Medical School and found a room we could rent with breakfast privileges.

I trained as a teacher, specializing in English, French, and also biology because I was planning to marry a doctor. I never taught biology; that was just as well. I never would have cleaned up the lab in time for the next class. English as a second language was not offered in those days; it would have been more useful than Shakespeare, but I loved Shakespeare.

Our first year in Rochester I taught junior high English and discovered that I wasn't a junior high teacher. The second year I worked in an office. I taught Sunday School that year and discovered how delightful second graders are. The last two years I was privileged to teach second grade in a fine city school.

Our friends and classmates were graduated from seminary and ready for their careers. Norm had a fourth year of med school, then three more years of internship and residency after med school, in order to become a general practitioner with some experience in surgery. At that time most of our mission hospitals were one-doctor institutions; the physician needed to turn his hand to whatever needed to be done. Specialization was not appropriate.

Now was the time to start a family. Bobby was born ten years after Pearl Harbor.

During residency in Detroit we finally completed the application process and were commissioned as missionaries of the American Baptist Foreign Mission Society (ABFMS). We met the board in New York City on Jan. 20, 1953, the day President Eisenhower was inaugurated. I was pregnant with Grace and wore a peplum dress that I hoped would hide my condition. I was mistaken.

We were excited about our assignment to the Chin Hills of Burma. The ABFMS had two mission stations in the Chin Hills, Falam in the north and Tiddim in the south, but no medical work. Our job— Norm's job—would be to establish a hospital at Haka, centrally located between Falam and Tiddim.

We took advantage of being in New York to see some of the sights. One day we journeyed to the United Nations buildings. Because we hadn't allowed enough time for the subway trips, we missed an appointment with Dr. Freas, a Congo missionary in the States at that time. Had we talked with him, we probably would have saved a year out of our lives.

Norm completed his residency by the end of 1953. That Christmas saw our little row house in Detroit very full, with my parents, Norm's parents, his brother and sister and brother's girlfriend all come to celebrate together. Most stayed to help with the move. The mothers took charge of the kitchen while Norm's sister, also named Grace, worked with us in the basement, recording each thing we put in a box to go overseas. Some friends, having read Gordon Seagrave's *Wastebasket Surgery*, donated used medical instruments. Grace inadvertently left out an "l" from "scalpel," so that her list of contents included "1 box scalpes."

Dr. Spock's book *Baby and Child Care,* the bible for new mothers, had warned me that moving was not good for a child right around two. Bobby had turned two December. Having the house full of relatives no doubt caused enough stress already, but worse was to come. A couple in our church generously offered to take Bobby and eight-month-old Grace for a day so we would be freer. We gladly accepted, not considering that the children really didn't know the couple at all. They seemed to have a good time, and the host couple brought them to the farewell party at church that night. So far, so good. In the middle of the night Bobby started crying, and we weren't able to wake him up completely so we could comfort him. Furthermore, there was no place to take him so he wouldn't disturb others. Every bedroom was full, and to go anywhere else we'd have to take him through the living room, where parents were sleeping, or trying to. I thought, "If he's this upset now, what will it be like when we actually move?"

Moving day did come. Our pastor stored the boxes ready for Burma in the parsonage basement. I don't remember what happened to the furniture, but everything else went in or on our little Ford, named Henry, of course. We packed the back seat full from the floor up to the backs of the front seats. In the middle, dividing the space in two, stood a vertical, folded card table, reaching almost to the ceiling. When we were ready to depart, we slipped a snow-suited child lying down on each side of the card table, we got into the front, and off we went. Imagine what would happen if we tried that now! But the little ones didn't seem to mind at all. As soon as we were in the car, just the four of us, Bobby settled down and enjoyed the actual move.

I'm sure our long-suffering parents stayed behind and cleaned up after us. What would we have done without them!

We were traveling to Berkeley, California, for one semester at Berkeley Baptist Divinity School. The trip didn't go very fast; dear old Henry required a present each day. Albuquerque is the place where we bought the new water pump. Going across the desert we purchased a desert water bag, but unfortunately we hung it in front of the radiator, making the coolant boil faster.

Finally we arrived in Berkeley, in time to start the spring semester. Grace celebrated her second Easter before her first birthday, as Easter came earlier the next year. The kids enjoyed playing with other small ones in the apartment building for married students. Norm took a full load of classes, including homiletics, while I remember a fascinating course in apologetics and an evening class in missions. I recall the prof asking us, "What will you do when you run out of love for the people you're working with?"

Usually willing to raise my hand, I answered, "I guess we ask God for a new supply."

We also took a course in linguistics at the University of Berkeley, with an exciting woman prof who talked about her friendship with the prince of Thailand. He knew many languages. Once she asked him, "Your highness, what language do you think in?"

"Mademoiselle," he replied. "I don't think!" Too many languages running around in his head.

Somewhere along the way I learned my first Burmese words, *"Bey go thwameley?"* It means, "Where are you going?" and I learned it as a greeting. Amazingly, people who know Burmese still recognize it when I say it! Of course I never learned anything to say after that.

Now why was that? When we had left Detroit for California, we'd thought we'd be sailing from the west coast. No, they sent us back east, speaking in churches along the way, to attend New Missionaries Conference in Meadville, Pennsylvania. That year the World Council of Churches met in Evanston, and we were blessed to hear some great world figures, including the literacy pioneer Frank Laubach and Canon Max Warren, head of the Church Missionary Society (CMS) in England, who taught our Bible study. What a privilege! For those of us who would be traveling through London—we had passage on the *Queen Mary* to Southampton and then on a P&O boat to Rangoon (Rangoon!)—he asked what we'd most like to do in London. One wife longed to see the queen, and Canon Warren promised to try to arrange that. We wanted to attend a Gilbert and Sullivan production; that would probably be easier to manage than seeing the queen. We didn't get to London that year, but Canon Warren wrote a special letter each Christmas to those green American missionaries he had taught, and many years later, when he had retired from the CMS and become a Canon of Westminster Abbey, we stayed overnight with him and his delightful wife at the Abbey. Our younger daughter's classmates didn't believe her when she said she'd slept at Westminster Abbey.

We never did see the *Queen Mary,* much less a P & O Boat. Burma did not grant us visas. While we waited, we lived alternately with Norm's folks in Jamestown, New York, and mine, near Utica, New York. When Christmas came and no visa, we decided we'd better start brushing up on the French we'd taken in college, because the next choice for us was the Belgian Congo. Now if we had talked with Dr. Freas that day two years before, he would have persuaded us to forget Burma and go to Congo. He was a great persuader.

Neither Jamestown nor Utica is a large city, but in each place our parents found a French tutor and someone else with whom we could practice French conversation. Our helpful mothers took care of the children so we could both have a lesson every day and study for the next day. Then the mission board sent us to Yale for a crash French course in the summer. We lived in half of a Quonset hut in a village built for students who were veterans. In the summer they were allowed to sublet. It was hot; the students would play hoses over the metal roofs of their homes, while the children splashed in little round pools. Every child's toys were marked with his name because everyone played with everyone else. We took the kids to a babysitter in the morning, then went to class. I did housework in the afternoon and studied in the evening. I haven't been so well organized since.

Back in Detroit I had entitled a deputation talk "We Don't Know Where We're Going, But We're on Our Way." How true that turned out to be! Finally on that September day in 1955, we were definitely, literally, geographically on our way—not directly to Congo but to Belgium for a year of study to prepare us to work in their colony. The four parents had waved good-by to us from the pier, with mixed feelings. They wanted us to go; we were fulfilling their dream as well as ours. But how they would miss us, especially my folks, because they had no other children to visit them! I found out much later that my mother had cried until Norm's mother finally told her, "That's enough, Adah."

CHAPTER TWO

Belgium

The ocean voyage passed smoothly. Experienced passengers described the Atlantic as a mill pond. One day the staff gave a party for the children, with balloons and professional photographs to keep the memory. We were surprised to have the steward announce, "Your bath is drawn, madam." One bathed first in sea water, and then rinsed off with a pail of fresh water provided for the purpose.

In the lounge one evening we were delighted to overhear a young Englishwoman say to an American friend, "You know, you really don't seem like an American." We knew she was paying her a compliment.

When the ship docked at Cherbourg, France, we were sent to a lounge to wait until called to go ashore in the lighter. People went out, and people went out, and finally we were almost alone. Fortunately we took the initiative just in time to avoid being left behind and going to Southampton by mistake.

Next lap: the boat train (the train that meets ships at the port) to Paris. With us were Joe and Ethel, another new American Baptist couple—in all we totaled seven couples and four single women

The party for the children on the *Queen Elizabeth* — how Bobby enjoyed it!

Yes, the *Queen Elizabeth!* Enjoying the deck — now Grace is having a good time too!

studying in Belgium that year—and a single woman who had already had a term in Congo. She described the French course we would take in Brussels. There were two sections, the *forte* or advanced class under the redoubtable professor Gilsoul, and the beginning, or *faible*, class, with a much easier prof. The French words mean literally "strong" and "weak." People dreaded M. Gilsoul but knew that they would learn a lot more if they studied under him.

We had supper at a nice little restaurant in the *Gare du Nord* before taking a night train to Brussels. The trip posed a problem for both our little children. There was no drinking water on board. One could buy pop or fizzy mineral water. Little Grace was thirsty but couldn't stand the fizzy stuff. She'd make a face and give up; then after a while thirst would make her take another drink, just as unsatisfactory. For Bobby the trouble came in the rest room. The toilet emptied directly onto the ground between the tracks. With the land rushing by at the bottom of that hole, he just couldn't do anything.

Arriving in Brussels, we must have been met by Mr. Coxill, whose job it was to take care of the many Protestant missionaries passing through Belgium on their way to the colony. Interesting for a tiny country to possess a colony many times larger than itself. Perhaps this would be a good place to speak up for the Belgians, who have been blamed for everything that ever went wrong in the Congo. Beginning in 1885, King Leopold I owned the Congo as his own personal possession, called, interestingly enough, the Congo Free State. It was free in the sense that other European countries didn't have to pay any customs duties. Leopold leased rights to companies that exploited the resources and the people. Vachel Lindsay's poem immortalized the custom of cutting off the hands of thieves. Surely the Belgian companies did not invent that method of punishment; it must have been practiced by chiefs before the Belgians ever came. No doubt people were much more willing to steal from the company than from an individual. At least, when we were there we found that people who would never steal

13

from each other saw nothing wrong with taking from an institution, a school or a hospital. Its resources must have seemed limitless.

In 1908 the Belgian parliament took over the colony, which then became the Belgian Congo. They really did a lot of things right. They just about stamped out sleeping sickness with their public health program and kept down malaria in the agglomerations by spraying. Christian missions started schools long before the government did, but the government subsidized the Catholic schools, Belgium being a 99% Catholic country. When a free-thinking government came into power, they didn't stop subsidizing the Catholic schools; they subsidized the Protestant ones as well. Seeing what happened in India, where the British gave higher education to a few and no education to many, the Belgians decided to bring everyone up together, emphasizing primary education for the masses and delaying higher education. One result was that the literacy rate in the Belgian Congo compared favorably with that in almost all other African countries at that time. Officials at different levels of government varied, of course, in their attitudes and actions, but in general the colony was well administered. Of course, it was a paternalistic system, doing many things for the Congolese but not with them.

Obviously we didn't know all that on our first morning in the very European city of Brussels, with its medieval town hall, cathedral, and green market. Mr. Coxill took us to a hotel, explaining, "You'll stay here until you find a place to live."

Studying the menu for our first noon meal, we ordered, *"Filet américain* with *sauce anglaise, s'il vous plaît."*

Fortunately the kind waitress informed us, *"Filet américain* is ground beef served raw." Why they would call it American we never did find out.

We found an apartment on the third floor of a typical Belgian building touching its neighbors with no space between. There was a

What a fun place for Bobby and Grace to play!

tiny balcony in front, over the sidewalk. Since the September weather was definitely cool and the apartment boasted no refrigerator, I used to keep my milk bottle on the balcony until the neighbor on the second floor informed me, "The neighbors don't appreciate your displaying a milk bottle on the balcony. There's a *cave* (basement) where things will stay cool." It seemed a long way to go for a bottle of milk.

Right across the street a kindergarten was located, taking children from three to five. How ideal for Bobby! That was my first experience of the very formal, regimented style of Belgian education. In class the children did interesting things like making applesauce, but I was not allowed to visit. When it was time to go home, the children lined up and met their parents in order.

Most of our fellow missionaries were in Brussels to take the colonial course, required for teachers who wanted to be certified by the government so their schools could receive government subsidies. Doctors and nurses, however, studied tropical medicine in Antwerp.

Norm commuted, taking the tram to the train station, a train to Antwerp, then another tram to the School of Tropical Medicine.

His studies started with a crash French course for foreigners, which had already begun when we arrived. The colonial course had not yet started, and I, along with our colleagues, took the placement exam, a *dictée de sélection*. Belgian and French people, perhaps Europeans in general, love dictation. I think dictating whole sentences is a much better way to test spelling than giving individual words, but they use a dictation to test language capability in general, judging that if you can write down what the professor said you probably understand it. It's very hard to get a good grade because every wrong letter or punctuation mark counts against you, a grammatical error counting a whole point out of ten. To my surprise, the *dictée* was much easier than the one we had been given at Yale. It came from an early lesson in the French text we had used in the States! It began: *La petite Hélène est malade.* "Little Helen is sick." Not surprisingly, I was placed in the coveted and dreaded *forte* class, but I never did meet the famous Prof. Gilsoul.

Norm came home one day and announced, "If I have to commute I'm not going to pass the course." So we moved to Antwerp. Bobby dropped out of kindergarten and I did not take the colonial course. We American doctors' wives in Antwerp tried a session with a tutor and a night school course for Flemish speakers, then settled down to just living in Antwerp.

I'll never forget our last night in Brussels. I thought I'd better wash the blankets by hand, in the bathroom, and hang them in the bathroom to dry. I have no idea what we slept under that night. The landlady lived in Paris but happened to be in the house at the time. Our bathroom was on the landing between two floors, and her bedroom stood under it on the landing below. In the night she woke up feeling what she first thought was a small animal on her bed. It turned out to be drops of water coming through the ceiling from my dripping blankets. Oh dear!

Our apartment in Antwerp occupied the ground floor. The landlady lived next door, but her daughter and family were in the basement below us. When we took a bath we went down there. A toilet hid in a tiny closet across the marble-floored hall from our apartment. To wash your hands you used the kitchen sink. There was, however, a *bidet* in the bedroom. We ignorant Americans made fun of the *bidet,* but it came in very handy. We euphemistically called it a foot-bath; it was intended for washing the bottom. I think it was big enough for bathing the tots.

Here the kitchen was located at the back of the house, facing a walled courtyard where I hung clothes and the children played in safety. The kitchen window included a window box both inside and outside. Not having a green thumb, I used the box as a refrigerator outside at first, and inside when the outside temperature got down to freezing.

Passing from the kitchen, where we ate, through the bedroom, where all of us must have slept, one came to the living room, which looked out on the Avenue of the Americas, a beautiful boulevard with trams going right by our door. Once Bobby had been in the kitchen watching snow come down in the back courtyard. Then he walked into the living room for some reason, looked out the front windows and remarked in surprise, "It's snowing out there too!"

Bobby had a little sister, but he really wanted a baby brother too. I pointed out that Bobby was still wetting the bed. "How would I have time to take care of you and Grace and a baby brother too?"

That afternoon Bobby woke up dry from his nap. I was congratulating him when the doorbell rang. The three-year-old asked hopefully, "Is that the baby brother?" Talk about instant gratification!

The neighbors had two boys, Jean-Paul, seven, and Jean-Jacques, five. Bobby turned four in December. He used to play with Jean-Jacques, but of course he knew very little French. Jean-Jacques would tell him to do something, and Bobby would reply, *"Oui, oui,"* but not understanding, he wouldn't do whatever it was. This got very frustrating for the five-year-old.

Grocery shopping went on every day—to the bakery to buy *pain gris,* literally "gray bread" but very tasty; to the butcher's to buy meat—they left the door open on the coldest winter days so customers would come in, and the personnel all got frostbite; to the grocery store for packaged items; to the outdoor market for vegetables. There were so many kinds of cabbage, and they were always the cheapest vegetables. Now the Belgians made a wonderful soup with all sorts of vegetables and followed it with meat and potatoes for their main meal. I had the meat and potatoes and vegetables at noon and made soup with the leftovers for supper. So-called red cabbage is actually purple, isn't it? And when you save the cooking water to use in soup, it's blue. Bobby got tired of cabbage; I started calling it by its French name, *chou.* One day he proclaimed, "I don't want any more cabbage or *chou.*"

You didn't have to make your own soup if you didn't want to. In Brussels I could take my pan to the corner store and buy a liter of soup. In Antwerp the soup cart came to the door, holding vats with two kinds of delicious soup to fill my pan. On a nearby corner we could watch people making French fries in a glass-walled kiosk on wheels, and buy some wrapped in a paper cone. My neighbor Mme Neal found it easier to make her own!

Norm's French professor was delightful. His wife would invite students and their wives to their lovely home for an evening. She showed us their fireplace, lined with white tiles, each one hand-painted and different from every other—even those that were all blackened with soot.

At Thanksgiving time the prof talked with these American doctors about that American holiday: *les pères pèlerins,* "Pilgrim fathers," and *la dinde,* "the turkey." Then he asked, "Does anyone know how to say 'stuffed turkey'?" Well, during our tutoring days we had learned that you don't translate "I'm full" literally in French. If you're a man it means, "I'm drunk"; for a woman, "I'm pregnant." Our tutor had taught us the refined way to express the idea of having eaten plenty: *rassasié.* Norm had asked, "How do you say 'stuffed'"? Well, it depends on what you're talking about. A cushion is *rembourré,* but a turkey may be *farcie.* Norm wowed the prof by properly describing a stuffed turkey.

The tropical medicine course included different professors for different subjects. Norm took me along for one lesson on languages of Congo. Final exams were difficult because the Belgians believed in oral exams. That meant the prof asked you one or a few questions, and if you weren't up on the subject he chose for you, too bad. We heard about one luckless missionary who had missed a class in one subject and neglected to borrow a classmate's notes for that day. The prof selected that material on that student's final, and the student had to repeat tropical medicine. Norm passed, and was certified on a higher level than some of his colleagues because he had studied Latin in high school!

While our friends in Brussels had two full semesters of class, Norm finished about the end of January but had to wait several weeks to hear the results. We used the time to do a little touring. The organist of my dad's church in New Hartford, New York, was Welsh and had invited us to visit his estate in Wales. We took the ferry to the white cliffs of Dover and rented a little Austin to travel around England and Wales. Now we saw London for the first time. We drove down through Sussex and Surrey, then west to Stratford-on-Avon, but we didn't see a Shakespeare play. It was cold in England in February. We found out that it doesn't do a bit of good to let your sixpenny heater work while you're out; it doesn't heat the room but works only by radiation. It warms you only if you're standing in front of it. In Stratford we were given bricks to keep our feet warm in bed. The bathroom was again on the landing, with a sign on the door in case a line formed: "There is another WC at the bottom of the garden." We Americans had visions of digging down through the snow to the bottom of the garden.

Eventually we arrived in Wales, with its beautiful, unpronounceable place names. The address of the organist's estate comprised no numbers, only a series of names. We drove through North Conway and eventually found it. I had envisioned something on a cliff, perhaps a little more modest than Daphne du Maurier's Manderley. The estate turned out to be half a house on a quiet residential street. We received a warm welcome. The next day we were taken to visit the castle and other sights, including what was billed as the smallest house in the world. There were two floors. We were told that the fisherman who had occupied the house was tall, so his legs stuck out the upstairs window. The neighboring women used to take advantage of him by hanging their laundry on the projecting lower extremities. The house actually existed; the story about it was something else again. Across the bay we visited Llandudno, with a statue of Alice in Wonderland.

With another couple we spent one day touring the Netherlands. I was surprised to find the country at least half Catholic. In the States you find rest rooms at gas stations; it was not so in the Netherlands. We had to stop at a restaurant or tea shop to attend to those needs. A missionary already in the Congo had asked us to buy her a light woolen blanket, so we looked for the proper store in the narrow streets of Amsterdam. It was easy to find the word "pure"— *zuiver*—but how to say "light"?

By the way, did you wonder why we learned French, not Belgian? There is no Belgian language. Belgium is made up of Walloons in the southeast, who speak French, and Flemings in the northwest, who speak Flemish. The Dutch say Flemish is a dialect of Dutch, but the Flemings are sure it's a separate language, and our friend and colleague Don told us it's the language closest to English. We did not try to learn it, although it's the language of Antwerp, and people there did not like to use French. (Our neighbors the Neals were an exception.) I tried very hard at the train station to ask for a round-trip ticket to Brussels in French good enough so I wouldn't be answered in English. One day Bobby remarked, "God knows all languages, even Flemish."

Back in the Netherlands, we finished the day driving through fishing villages in the northwestern provinces. It felt cozy to be able to look in through undraped windows that went down almost to the floor and see families at their evening meal.

For our last trip we rented a Renault and drove first to Paris. It was so cold! We'd drive until our feet felt freezing, then walk a while till our hands got too cold. Bobby lost his cap in the Seine. We visited Notre Dame but couldn't climb way up on account of glare ice on the stairs. Versailles was amazing; it went on and on. Louis XIV slept in a very short bed. People weren't as tall in those days, but also I understand they sort of sat up in bed. Then the gardens went on and on too, with lots of statuary. Finally we got to the Grand Trianon and the Petit Trianon, where Marie Antoinette put on plays. Too bad Bobby was too young to remember. When he was in high school I tried to tell him about Versailles for a test he had to take the next day, but he was so sleepy his eyes glazed over and nothing penetrated.

CHAPTER THREE

To the Congo by Freighter

Our American Baptist colleagues came from Brussels to the pier to see us off on the *Armand Grisard.* Since Norm was a doctor, we were allowed to travel by freighter. We never found out who Armand had been, but the ship carried a cargo of ferry boats and salt fish. With us went John, another American doctor, with his wife and little girl. John had grown up in the Congo, so his experience and knowledge of the Kikongo language were invaluable. Becky was a little younger than our Grace. Grace wore her hair long and her dresses short; Mennonite Becky did just the opposite.

As soon as we had unpacked in our staterooms, Jeanne suggested, "Let's ask where we can find an ironing board and iron our clothes."

"That's a good idea," I assented. I never would have thought of it myself! The room they showed us was small and hot, and I felt a little seasick, but it didn't last.

There were two other passengers, an American single woman missionary and a Belgian woman. It must have been lonely for the Belgian: I don't remember our reaching out to her at all. How selfish of us! The American woman loved children and was happy to watch ours. And I was happy to let her. During that trip of two weeks or so I wrote 75 letters, put our tiny grayscale photos from Europe in an album, and gave myself a Tip-Toni. Photos taken since that time never made their way into albums, our correspondence is woefully neglected, and I have never again given myself a perm. The children had a ball exploring the ship and did not fall overboard. Once Bobby was allowed to hold the wheel that steers the ship. We were given a photo to prove it.

Life on a freighter was quite luxurious for the passengers. The meals always included several courses, with a selection of cheeses just before dessert, and coffee last of all in solitary splendor. A small meal was served mid-morning. The last evening they brought out Baked Alaska flambé. I was so disappointed! The brandy they had poured over it and ignited spoiled the flavor.

Actually the food was too rich. Grace and I both developed diarrhea two or three days before we landed in the Congo. I wondered if we couldn't just keep on enjoying the food and worry about the diarrhea later, but the good doctor limited us to white foods—potatoes and rice, primarily. We didn't really recover till we were eating wholesome Swedish food at the mission guest house in Matadi.

In the meantime we had stopped in the Canaries—not on Ténérife, as most ships did, but at Las Palmas on Palm Sunday! We saw the Palm Sunday procession, with a number of barefoot men carrying a representation of Jesus on the donkey. We were impressed with the wealth of the Catholic Church—lots of gold in the church buildings—and the poverty of the people, some of whom lived in caves. And we took pictures of goats. We had taken pictures of goats in Switzerland, which we visited after Paris, and we would take more pictures of goats in the Congo. Goats seem to be quite ubiquitous.

We made port again at Pointe Noire in what was then French Equatorial Africa. There are now two countries called Congo, the former French Congo (Republic of Congo) and the former Belgian

Congo (DRC or Democratic Republic of the Congo), across the river—very confusing. This was our first sight of Africa and Africans, our first hearing of Kikongo.

We were still on the ship on Easter Sunday. John held a service for the African crew. They all took off their shoes before worship.

Grace had her third Easter on shipboard, before her third birthday.

April 2, 1956, we made our way some 100 km up the Congo River to the port of Matadi. That's as far as the first Portuguese explorers got. Upstream from Matadi there are rocks and rapids; the river doesn't become navigable again till Kinshasa, which was called Leopoldville in those days, after the Belgian king who owned the country for 23 years. *Matadi* means rocks. The men unloading our freighter sang or chanted, *"Rrrhaa!";* maybe it corresponded to "Yo ho, heave ho!"

Matadi ascends from the river. The post office and government buildings and hotels occupy a level well above the docks, and then the streets climb up and up before you arrive at the Swedish mission—simple, clean, welcoming—our first taste of life in the Congo. It was good to see our first indoor lizard in the guest house living room with other people about, who assured us a lizard was good to have around, as it ate insects. This one was the small white kind, almost transparent. Years later Bobby's little brother would watch them crawling on the outside of the window screen and try to mark one's white belly through the screen so he would know it was his.

At the post office I encountered my first example of discrimination. There were two lines, a short one for whites and a long one for Congolese. I knew I should not accept the privilege, but I justified taking advantage of it because my time was limited. Did I think their time didn't count?

"We'd better buy enough bread and a few other things here to carry us through our first week in the bush," John told us. So we did. What did we know? On the day of our departure the Swedish missionary in

25

charge of the guest house made us lunch to take on the train, including green bananas. They were ripe and overripe by afternoon.

The train was scheduled to arrive at Sona Bata, 50 miles before the capital city of Leopoldville, at 2:30, but it was rainy season and there had been a washout. We waited four hours. Then we were going again. Bobby looked eagerly for villages along the way. At first they were all well removed from the railroad right of way, but when he finally spotted one he wanted to get off the train and tell the villagers they needed to wear shoes. We had impressed upon him the necessity of wearing shoes in that country where hygiene may be minimal and walking barefoot presents various hazards. He wanted to share his protective knowledge. A couple of years later, at Sona Bata, he would rush into the house exclaiming, "There's a boy here who's not Congolese!"

"Not Congolese? He isn't black?"

"Oh, he's black all right, but he's a shoe boy! He wears shoes like us!"

CHAPTER FOUR

Sona Bata

The train arrived at Sona Bata at 6:30. By that time it was dark. I turned to the Belgian in our compartment, who had befriended these newcomers to the country, and asked, "Is this really Sona Bata?"

He assured me it was. The station had no electricity, only a lantern. We disembarked with our luggage; Norm asked for the stationmaster. *"C'est moi,"* replied the man. "It's me," or "I'm it."

Norm replied, "I'm the new doctor."

"Tiens, tiens!" replied the *chef de gare.* That translates, "Well, well," or in this case I think, "Well, whaddaya know about that!"

The Sona Bata missionaries knew we were coming but didn't know what day to expect us. The stationmaster sent word up the hill to the mission station by means of a boy, I imagine, and in due time our senior missionary, Roland, arrived in a Combi (Comb-bee)—Volkswagen bus—to pick us up. He had been working on the electricity in our house; Sona Bata possessed a generator that was operated from 6:00 p.m. till 9:00. Roland had inadvertently cut off the current for the whole station.

It's possible that no other missionary was ever greeted exactly the way we were that evening. Ordinarily, when new missionaries arrived, the school boys and girls were brought out to sing to them. We had come during Easter vacation—no school kids around. But Norm was the long-awaited new doctor. Sona Bata had seen our first American Baptist hospital in the Congo, with Dr. King in charge, before we were born, and our first Protestant nurses' training school. Dr. Tuttle and his British colleague had moved that school to Kimpese, where there was more room to expand. The school at Sona Bata now gave two years of training, turning out something between practical nurses and nurses' aides. After the departure of the four-year school, Sona Bata had continued with one doctor, and for the past six months a missionary nurse had been in charge.

When the Combi reached the top of the hill, we were told we were outside our house, the doctor's house, separated from the hospital by a tennis court. Of course we couldn't see anything, but from the darkness came singing. The hospital staff, patients' relatives, and patients were standing on our lawn singing to welcome us.

In the morning a wizened little woman came over, took Norm's hands, and knelt in front of him. Of course we couldn't understand her words, but we gathered the sense of them: "Thank God you've come."

The early years of mission work in the Congo—the late 1800s—were terribly difficult. Few missionaries lived to return to their home country after one term. They died of malaria, sleeping sickness, or some tropical infection they had never developed resistance to. Language had to be learned with no manual and no informant who knew the language you were coming from. Living conditions were starkly primitive, and missionary efforts were met with suspicion.

In recent years missionaries have again met with suspicion and mistrust, to say nothing of riots and civil wars. Runaway inflation, political instability, and collapsed infrastructure have made it very hard to carry on the work.

We arrived in the Congo in the halcyon days. Missionaries were welcomed and appreciated. Boys and, increasingly, girls were eagerly sent to school. Life went along on a pretty even keel. There were problems, of course, but in comparison with those who went before and those who came after, we had it easy.

Back to April 4, 1956. Eventually the songs came to an end and the Combi moved on, straight up to the steps of a duplex shared by Eva and Esther. Esther was the nurse who had carried the whole responsibility of the 100-bed hospital since the doctor had left and who would continue to carry a good deal of it as Norm studied Kikongo and learned the ropes. Eva, an experienced missionary, directed both the primary school and the teachers' training school. During the brief time that we waited down at the station, Roland or someone, probably Esther, had alerted the hospital to our arrival and Eva had fixed supper for us. We enjoyed a royal welcome.

After supper we were introduced to our house by the light of a kerosene lamp or two. In our large bedroom stood a 3/4 bed and a single hospital bed. There was a small bedroom for the two children, but the place seemed so new and strange we decided to share the 3/4 bed and put the children in the single bed, one at the head and the other at the foot. We had done that trick while visiting England. Of course the weather here was hot; we probably put only a sheet over them, and it wasn't tucked in well enough; the bed was pretty high, and the floor was made of concrete. Grace fell out and met people the next day with a swollen lip.

Morning came about 6:30. Daylight allowed us to explore our new home. Early missionary bungalows were spacious and airy. Our square house was divided into four parts: living room, dining room, bedroom, and the other quarter divided into a long bathroom and a walk-through closet. A screened veranda went all the way around the house. Behind the veranda in back stood a four-room cookhouse: sink kitchen on the left, with the storeroom behind; stove kitchen on the right, with a laundry room behind. That was the original house. In the early days Congo missionaries sent their babies back to the States for health reasons, but after one brave missionary wife pioneered keeping children on the field with their parents, another bedroom was needed. In this case, a corner of the veranda next to the bathroom was closed in for the children's room. Another corner had been walled in for the doctor's home office. Every room opened onto the veranda. I counted 11 outside doors. That first term we never locked any of them unless we were going to be away overnight. It was a good place to live. The living room included a fireplace, but we almost never used it. I had supposed that dry season would be hot, but the mornings could be surprisingly chilly. However, who has time to sit around the fireplace in the morning?

Our senior missionaries had made up a meal schedule so we didn't have to cook for ourselves the first week. We didn't need all that bread we'd bought in Matadi! The next year a new couple came, and we were one of the host families. As Orville and Virginia left after the first meal, they thanked us.

"You'll be back here on Thursday," I assured them.

"Oh, I hope not!" Orville burst out. We laughed, realizing he meant, "We don't want to be a burden."

During that first week we got acquainted with the beautiful station of Sona Bata, built on seven hills, like Rome. Two of them, near the hospital, held the dormitories for male and female nursing students and hospital staff. Our senior nurse had been trained when students were required to be married. Each man needed a wife to grow food and cook for him. He had had five years of primary school and then five years of nurses' training at Sona Bata, after which he performed like a doctor, diagnosing and treating patients and performing minor surgery. Now the four-year students at Kimpese completed nine grades before entering nurses' training; ours had had six, and they were young and unmarried.

Missionaries called the two main hills Prayer Hill and Pill Hill. We, of course, lived on Pill Hill. The other hill housed the church, Eva's two schools and a homemaking school for girls, and the homes of those who worked there plus students' dormitories. I preferred to call it Pulpit Hill, contending that just as much prayer went up from the medical side. In the valley between those hills stood the precious generator, which supplied electricity from 6:00 to 9:00 p.m.

Roland and Lillian occupied the big, light, airy house nearest the road that went by both our mission station and the village of Sona Bata. Another large house on that side was called the Coop. It had been made for two single missionaries. Only Madelyn was occupying it now. She had charge of the homemaking school and did me the great favor of transferring her cook to our employ. He had previously been a painter at the hospital; she had trained him to cook. Before I started being on my own for meals, with Kikongo lessons beginning the same day, I took her three small pieces of paper on which I had written words and phrases I'd need to know those first few days. She filled in the Kikongo equivalents.

Right away I ran into a snag with Tata Nzeza. Dear Eva came over to help me get started. The first thing I said to the new cook was: "Go get drinking water." We had running water in our houses, but the spring water was considered better for drinking.

31

The ex-painter informed Eva (since I wouldn't understand), "I don't fetch water, I'm a cook. She needs a boy (helper) to get water."

Tactfully Eva suggested, "Since she doesn't have a boy yet, perhaps you could go for water this one time."

He agreed, I breathed a sigh of relief, and Eva went back to her work.

When Tata returned from the spring I consulted my little sheets and told him in the Kikongo on my little paper, "Mop the floor."

He replied, *"Ka mambu ko; si ya sukula."* What did he mean? I knew *sukula*; it was the word I'd used for "mop" (wash). But what did the rest of the words signify? Was he refusing again? I hotfooted it as fast as I could go to Eva's house, repeating all the way, *"Ka mambu ko; si ya sukula."*

Eva and Esther got a good laugh when I burst breathlessly into their living room saying, "He says, *'Ka mambu ko; si ya sukula.'* What does that mean?"

"It means, 'All right. I'll mop.'" Madelyn had given me *"Ka diambu ko"* for "all right," literally "no problem," but how was I to know that *mambu* was the plural of *diambu* and was used the same way?

After that Tata Nzeza and I got along all right. He didn't read, so if I wanted him to make something Madelyn hadn't taught him I had to show him how. The first time I wanted pancakes I said the word in English—no comprehension. I tried the French word, *crêpes*—no.

Then I started making them in front of him, and the light dawned: "Oh, *panakukasi.*" Kikongo seldom puts two consonants together and ends every word with a vowel, so "pan-cake-s" had to have three more syllables.

I think of two incidents connected with Tata Nzeza. Once I threw away a doll of Grace's that had lost a leg or an arm.

He picked it out of the wastebasket and asked, "Could I take this home to my little girl?"

"Yes, indeed, Tata," I replied.

Later I told Grace, "Tata Nzeza's little girl doesn't have any dolls."

She responded immediately, "I'll give her some."

Much later, on a more primitive station, Grace was attending second grade in the local school. The teacher remarked one day, "You girls should really have three dresses: one for school, one for work and play, and one for church."

Grace came home troubled: "I have lots more than three."

Once Tata Nzeza came to work upset. Someone had put a hex on his house, he informed me. He had found a bunch of grass in front of the house that he was sure was a fetish intended to harm his family. He wanted to move from his concrete block house to a grass hut. I couldn't change his mind. I hadn't realized he was not a Christian. After that I talked to him about Jesus, but I'm sadly sure his life was not changed as a result of that conversation.

After a week to get settled at Sona Bata, Norm left for a month's *stage* at the Evangelical Medical Institute in Kimpese, called by the French initials IME. This was the medical complex founded by the two doctors who had been at Sona Bata and looked for more room to expand. From the train we had seen some of the buildings; now Norm was to have his Congo internship there, learning how to practice medicine in tropical Africa. Toward the end of the time the children and I joined him. That night I woke up crying out, having dreamed that a snake was coming in through the ventilation opening high up near the ceiling.

That same weekend a patient named Rémy was brought in. Rémy was such a fine, gifted Christian teacher that senior missionary Mary had found a way to send him to Belgium for normal school, a teacher training institute on a junior college level. He was the first of our mission to go that far in education. He had returned from Belgium shortly after we arrived there. The missionaries were thrilled to have a well-trained Congolese teacher taking over some of the courses.

But now he was desperately ill. IME was the best hospital around, but in spite of all efforts he died. I remember praying for a resurrection!

Autopsy showed that a parasite had localized in the brain tissue—very unusual. That was the scientific explanation. Many local people believed that sorcery had been used against him because he had got too far ahead of his fellows. Americans admire heroes who stand head and shoulders above the crowd. In Congo you don't want to stand out.

Years later I was looking for a student who could take charge of the PE class that day, since the teacher was sick. I stuck my head inside the classroom door and called out, "Who's the best soccer player?"

The answer came back, "We're all identical."

After his time in Kimpese Norm had another week or two of internship in Leopoldville, the capital, also the headquarters of the American Baptist Foreign Mission Society in the Congo. We joined him there too and got acquainted with the missionaries in the city. I went up to someone's house one day and knocked on the door. The missionary called out, *"Nani?"*

I replied, "It's not Nani, it's me." That was how I learned that *nani* means "who."

Back at Sona Bata Norm got into the routine of hospital work, saving half the day for Kikongo study as long as Esther was there. Rémy's death made a difference at our station. Educational missionaries Jim and June were transferred from Sona Bata to Nsona Mpangu to take Rémy's place. I don't know what they did about other courses, but I was asked to teach sixth grade French. At that time the Belgian colonial government was trying something new: They separated out the best students finishing fifth grade and made an elite sixth grade of those preparing to go on to secondary education, which then consisted of two three-year sections. We had no secondary school at our station. Nsona Mpangu had the first section. In our area only Kimpese offered a complete high school education. It was a union station, where several missions worked together in educational and agricultural work as well as medical.

Grace had celebrated her third birthday shortly after arriving at Sona Bata. Before Jim and June left she enjoyed playing with their Betty Sue and admiring her new baby sister. One day she reported, "Betty Sue's baby is all made of little stuff."

My class came early in the morning. One day I came home to find the children at the breakfast table joyfully throwing the dishes at each other. I had asked Tata Nzeza to watch them, but unfortunately I used the wrong verb, one that means to look at rather than to supervise. So he obediently watched them throw the dishes around.

We spent over three years at Sona Bata. Norm was very busy, the only doctor for the 100-bed hospital, also in charge of the nursing school and several rural dispensaries which required regular visits. Kimpiatu, the head Congolese nurse, was an invaluable help with learning the language, learning the customs, understanding what was going on and just listening when Norm needed to share problems. Once every three months Norm made a surgical visit to Boko, a mission station a long, difficult day's journey away. Boko had a hospital run by a missionary nurse but no doctor. I remember complaining to that nurse, "I'm so slow."

She responded, "I am too, so I have to work long hours." All right, Jean, that's what you do about it.

Norm was a slow, painstaking surgeon and a good, patient teacher. When our second-year nursing class was to graduate we had equal numbers of girls and boys. The girls excelled! Norm had no time to

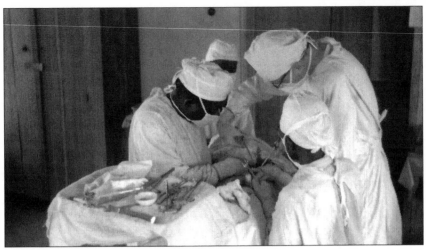

Norm and his team of nurses in surgery

prepare his speech. He asked the Holy Spirit for help, and the Spirit gave him a fine message.

Missionaries would come from Leopoldville to have their babies. Norm delivered seven missionary babies our first term, all girls. The most exciting was Tonda.

Norm congratulating the second-year nursing class

Mwesi, our nursing graduate on her wedding day

Don and Betsy came to the Congo two years after we did. They were assigned to Nsona Mpangu, a station downriver from us. It was the successor to Mbanza Manteke, the very first American Baptist mission station in the Congo. The Nsona Mpangu hospital did not have a doctor. Betsy was almost seven months pregnant and had a history of losing babies either just before they were born or just after. It was thought that Don and Betsy, with three children already, should stay at a station with a doctor, i.e., Sona Bata.

Yes, of course. But where would they stay? The Coop seemed a good idea, since it had more rooms than one single missionary would need. Well, no. Sharing a house with another single woman was one thing. Sharing it with a couple and three children was another. Sorry, but no.

Well, how about George's house? George was a single missionary in his early 20's, an exception to the usual practice of sending people 25 and over. He had been sent out to care for all the mission trucks and radios. We had eight stations at that time. Each possessed at least one or two trucks. Five had radios. It meant a lot of road travel and a lot of responsibility. It also involved problems that didn't normally occur in the States—communication problems. English, French, Kikongo? Does he really understand? Do I understand what he's saying? Availability—or unavailability—of parts. A worldview that does not include the idea of routine maintenance when nothing is broken yet. And the fearfully and wonderfully made roads of the Congo. George was very good at his job, but once he dreamed all the trucks on the eight stations were broken down at once.

George was living in a large house that later became the station pastor's. And he was away a lot. Wouldn't that be a good place for Don and Betsy? Well, no. It contained lots of radio equipment. George was not about to welcome children aged eight, four, and eighteen months into that house.

In the end Maurice and Judy invited Don and Betsy to share their duplex. It was the house where Eva and Esther had been when we came to Sona Bata. It had a common living room, dining room, and kitchen. On each side was an apartment for a single woman: office, bedroom, and bath. Maurice and Judy, with two boys and two girls, were occupying it. But the boys went to school in Leopoldville. The rest of the family would use one side of the house and give Don and Betsy, whose son would also be going to school in Leopoldville, the other side.

Somehow it worked. Tonda was indeed born two months early, but she survived and thrived. About the same time Judy had a miscarriage, so it was we who temporarily moved into George's house while ours held Norm's three missionary patients. I don't remember how we kept George's precious electronic stuff safe from our five- and four-year olds, but nothing untoward happened to it.

⚬❦⚬

After that first French class on Pulpit Hill, I taught French and math to our nursing students. I remember telling one girl, "Denise, you'll never make a nurse if you don't learn the multiplication table." I doubt she ever learned it, but she turned into a very good scrub nurse.

Bobby started kindergarten at home with the Calvert course, which I found excellent. In first grade he went to the local school (in Kikongo) in the morning and worked with me in the afternoon. I thought he was quite poetic. One morning he woke up earlier than usual, when it was just light. He looked out the window and exclaimed, "Isn't it beautiful! Nobody has woke up yet. There the road is, waiting for the people."

That makes me think of Christmas at Sona Bata. It started earlier than that, while it was still dark. Someone would come out of his house and start singing a Christmas carol. As other people and families heard, they would come out and join the singer. Gradually the group got larger and larger. Other groups would come from the other hills, and the whole population would arrive at the church for a sunrise Christmas service. Jesus is born!

One day Bobby was to dictate a story to me. He showed no signs of ever stopping, so finally I told him, "That's the end of the page, Bobby—no more room." I considered his story very good for a kindergartener and sent copies to both sets of grandparents.

One grandmother wrote back, "That's a wonderful story! I'm sure Bobby will grow up to be a writer or a preacher—somebody who uses words well."

The other grandmother responded, "I'm sure he'll improve as he grows older."

It was a slow 50 miles from Sona Bata on the dirt road to Leopoldville. During the dry season the road would fill up with sand, and eventually workers would shovel it out, off to the side. Over time this made part of the route a sunken road between dirt banks lined with trees. Now a Belgian company started paving the road. They made a contract with the Sona Bata hospital to treat all their workers. It made a good, dependable source of income for the hospital. We came to know a French couple working with the construction company. Their headquarters were nearby, and we exchanged visits. I made the mistake of serving them steak and French fries. Never try to serve someone their specialty when you can't do it very well. We enjoyed the couple, and they were very patient with our French. They invited us to their home, and I meant to say, "That would be great!" I thought of using the French word, *épatant,* for which we'd been given the translation "swell." Remember that word? But unfortunately, instead of *épatant* I said *épouvantable,* which translates "dreadful, horrible, appalling"! Madame graciously never turned a hair.

She wasn't so gracious with everyone, though. They showed us a little home movie her husband had made. They were walking along a path behind some Congolese women. The Frenchman carefully filmed his wife managing to give a little kick to the woman walking in front of her. Now why would she do that? I once saw a boy show his kid brother how to give a little kick to their sister as she went up the stairs ahead of them. Why would the Frenchwoman want to act like a pesky brother? Was she bored with no French neighbors, only Belgians, perhaps Flemings who scorned speaking French?

Then she and her husband showed off her clever trick to these Americans. They must have been proud of it! It was a good joke. We wanted to get acquainted with our Congolese neighbors. The company building the road treated their Congolese employees fairly, meeting their needs. This couple apparently wanted to make fun of them. We didn't say anything.

⤬

Norm took the children and me on one of his dispensary trips. The nearest dispensary was at a palm oil factory, very interesting. They used the debris from the palm nuts to stoke their boilers—sustainable energy! Norm checked the nurse's supply of medicines, saw patients, and talked with the nurse about his work. In order to help with one mental patient's diagnosis, Norm asked him to count to three. The man obediently recited, *"Mosi, zole, tatu."* Apparently he thought that was something the doctor really wanted to hear, because for the rest of the afternoon he would keep turning up saying, *"Mosi, zole, tatu."*

To get to the next dispensary Norm took a shortcut he had heard about. It turned out to be a long cut and very bumpy. At one point we came to two cemeteries. On the left was a traditional cemetery, with a plate, a lantern, or another useful item on each grave. They were for the spirit's life in the afterworld. Each object had a hole punched in it so it wouldn't be stolen for life in this world. On the other side stood a Christian cemetery with gravestones, some quite large and ornate and painted different colors. Five-year-old Bobby took one disgusted look and announced, "It isn't right to break up a road and then decorate it!"

Bobby had a small truck with a crane, which we had given him in Belgium. Another boy was playing with a hoop—the rim of a discarded bicycle wheel. They happily exchanged toys, to the satisfaction of both.

Our ocean freight included 40 barrels and boxes, and they arrived six months after we did, held up in customs at Matadi because they included a still for making distilled water for the hospital. Customs wanted all sorts of documents, including a photograph of the still. How do you take a picture of an apparatus housed in a box that you aren't permitted to have until you've submitted the photo? They also

Bobby admired the other boy's hoop

wanted to know what we were going to use it for. Our mission treasurer suggested, "Why, to make that good ole moonshine down in the holler."

Among the things we had packed were sundresses for Grace. The little square bodices didn't always cover everything, and sometimes she felt a bit embarrassed, but on the other hand, as she pointed out, "It makes it easier to nurse my dolls." She knew how because she saw the Congolese women nursing their babies.

Trucks and people had to cross the river by ferry

Our Congolese guide and helper, Grace, Bobby, and Norm crossing on the ferry

One day Norm started suffering severe back pain, which he eventually diagnosed as a herniated disc. He took to his bed. But the next night a bad accident occurred on our newly paved road. As a Belgian had predicted once in our living room, "People will drive on it as if it were an *autobahn,* but it isn't." Two trucks loaded with men,

Unloading our much-anticipated ocean freight onto our house veranda

women and children ran into each other head-on. Thirty people were brought in to the hospital. Norm got on his bicycle, rode it to the hospital, and leaned on it as he examined the patients.

The following day we drove—I drove with poor Norm flat on his back in the truck that we euphemistically termed our ambulance— southwest on the main road, away from the capital, to the big union hospital at Kimpese, which boasted a missionary orthopedist. The short, stocky doctor hoisted tall Norm on his back and jounced him in an effort to put the disc back in place. It didn't work. Then Norm had to endure the trip back to Sona Bata. The road was paved from Sona Bata to the capital but only a short distance in the other direction. From there on it was full of ruts and holes and bumps. How I wished I could drive as smoothly as Norm!

Eventually he ordered a back brace from the States and wore it until we went on furlough. In the States the orthopedist commanded, "Take that thing off and throw it away. I've gotten hod carriers back to work!"

As the months went by we understood more and more of what we heard in church. Sometimes the pastor would preach; another time it might be a teacher, a nurse, or a mason. Anyone could be called on to pray; no one declined. The preacher kept the congregation involved by starting a sentence and letting the people finish it. If he thought they might not be able to, he'd say the whole sentence and then repeat the first part. Once one of our nurses remarked, "I just wished he'd call on me to pray so I could fill out what was lacking in his sermon."

One very sharp teacher was a man named Lulendo. His son was about the same age as our Bobby and they played together. Most of Bobby's friends were a little older and made allowances for this little white kid. It was good for him to have one peer who gave as good as he took. Lulendo preached one time on the subject *"Kulumuka."* The word means "come down." Jesus said it to Zaccheus when he was up in the tree. Tata Lulendo told his compatriots, "We love to climb a tree and see what's going on. Anybody who starts a new sect gets lots of followers. We need to come down from the tree and commit ourselves."

One day I heard that one of the women had lost a child. I asked a nursing student to take me to the woman's home. She was there, and I tried in my limited Kikongo to comfort her. Later Tata Kimpiatu, who sometimes served as our language informant, heard about it and asked the student, "What did Mama Abell do there?"

"She exhorted her."

"I didn't know she knew that much Kikongo."

I wonder what I said. I wonder what the woman made of it. At least I paid her some attention.

In those days the Congo was still a Belgian colony. In 1958 Brussels hosted Expo 58, the first world's fair after World War II. There was a Congo pavilion, and the Belgian government brought some Congolese each month to act as docents. Kimpiatu was one of those chosen. Before he left he confided, "I'm afraid I'll be hungry with no manioc in Belgium."

When he returned he looked well fed. I told him so, and he admitted, "There were lots of other good things to eat."

Besides Kikongo and one or two other Bantu languages, he knew French and English, but there were visitors to the Expo who knew none of those. Kimpiatu described how they would ask through gestures, "Did the sun burn you that color?"

And nurse Kimpiatu would reply through gestures, "No, I came out of my mother's womb this way."

"On the way home," he told us, "I prayed the plane along till we'd crossed the Mediterranean. Then I figured the pilot could manage from there on, so I went to sleep."

When Norm went to Leopoldville he would visit the dispensary next to the Baptist Church in Kintambo, one of the sections of the city. This dispensary was in the capable hands of Mama Mattie, one of the first two female Congolese nurses, trained at Sona Bata under Dr. King when the first nursing school was very new. While Norm checked out what she was doing, the church women were having their meeting in the sanctuary. I was along on one trip, so I went in and sat in the back in time to hear one of the women praying for the doctor. "Give him wisdom and patience and love," she asked.

I thought, "What a good prayer!" We often found ourselves praying, "Lord, help us get through all this work that needs to be done," but

Mama Mattie and her children

46

she was praying for what was really important: wisdom and patience and love.

Much later I found out that the baby layettes American Baptist women sent over in White Cross to that dispensary were given only to those mothers who belonged to the church. I didn't think that was right. Mama Mattie explained, "We were afraid there wouldn't be enough for us if we gave them to everyone." It still wasn't right, but didn't I do the same thing? If I bought bananas at the market and on the way home someone asked me for one, I wouldn't give it because by the time I got home they would all be gone. But I could afford to get more, and maybe the people who asked couldn't.

We had known an Africa where only two countries were independent; all the rest were colonies of the UK or France or Spain or Portugal or Germany or Italy or Belgium. Now things were changing. In 1959 France gave autonomy to its African colonies. Germany and Italy had lost their colonies in WWII. The Belgians had had no plans to change the status of their colony, but with the new ferment for freedom they began to draw up a plan for independence in 30 years. That was too slow. All right, four years. The first elections were held for burgomasters (mayors) for the various sections of Leopoldville. And then it became clear that the Congolese were not willing to wait four years. Belgium was weary of war and did not want conflict with the colony it thought it had treated so well. Independence Day was set for June 30, 1960. Remember, the only elected officials were those burgomasters in the capital city. Who would replace all the Belgians in government posts? Who had the training? Who had any experience? I remember asking Lulendo, "Do you think the country's ready for independence?"

"Wouldn't you want to be free?" was his reply.

The church was already well on the way to independence. In 1956, just a few months after our arrival, we attended the last missionary conference, at which everyone looked eagerly at the blackboard that showed who would be going to what station for the coming year. There were always changes because some missionaries went on furlough each year and needed to be replaced. Distribution of the money sent out for the work was also handled there. Of course, needs always exceeded the supply, so competition was hot. Which station, which work needed the money more than another? Whatever anyone else said, one missionary would always counter, "Have you seen the boys' dorms at Sona Bata?" The following year and from then on, these matters would be discussed at *Mbundani*, the gathering of Congolese leaders. A few missionaries were included.

Two topics came up at that missionary conference that were of special significance to us. The Salk vaccine for polio had just come out in the States. Should we have some sent to the Congo so our children could be vaccinated? New missionary Jean Abell raised her little hand and suggested, "Since two of our doctors (Freas and Osterholm) have contracted polio, shouldn't we vaccinate adults as well as children?"

The idea was accepted, and the Abells became responsible for receiving the vaccine and seeing that it stayed cold on its journey to the other stations. A little later it would have been easy to send the vaccine by MAF (Mission Aviation Fellowship), but MAF didn't come to the Congo till after independence. Of course Norm vaccinated the Sona Bata missionary community first. One day I unthinkingly asked him at the table, "Are you going to shoot the missionaries today?"

Later a troubled little boy asked me, "Is Daddy really going to kill the missionaries?" Thank goodness he asked!

We took Boko's vaccine by truck, packed in a thermos bottle with ice cubes. Unfortunately the road was so bumpy that the bouncing ice cubes broke the delicate glass of the thermos. Fortunately, and somewhat to our surprise, we were able to stop at a town that had a store with both thermos bottles and ice. Now we knew we had to crush the ice before putting it in the bottle.

The other one-time question concerned the education of our children. The Presbyterians had a school for missionary children (or kids, also known as MKs) at Lubondai, near the middle of the country. American Baptists partnered with them in the high school; our children were paying guests in the elementary school. Now the baby boom or perhaps the influx of missionaries—our class of American Baptists was the largest ever to go to the Congo—had caught up with them, and they informed us that there might not be room for our children when their parents were ready to send them. What should we do? Should we start our own school for American Baptist MKs? It seemed very parochial. The MKs whose parents lived in Leopoldville had been going to the local Belgian school and getting along all right. Should we establish a hostel where children from the bush could live in the city and go to that school? It was a difficult decision, with lots to be said on both sides. Eventually we decided on the second alternative. Reidar and Sigrid, new missionaries just coming out, would be the first hostel parents, with, I think, seven boys and two girls. It's better to start working in a second language as young as possible. The Leopoldville parents recommended that we teach our children first grade at home so they'd get a start reading and writing English and then send them to first grade in the French language Belgian school. Since European education tended to be at least a year ahead of ours in academics, they would be able to skip a grade when they went back to the States.

Bobby was homeschooled; he could take as long as he needed on his work. That was a mistake. To this day he has trouble with deadlines because he's very painstaking.

I had vowed I would not send a child of mine away to school unless he wanted to go. Bobby wanted to go to Leopoldville to school. Visiting the city was fun; why not go to school there? I tried to teach him some French, but he wasn't interested. He'd learn it when the time came.

The time came. We were given a long list of books and notebooks he had to have, along with a schoolbag. Each book and notebook must be covered with blue paper which you bought along with the books. Bobby proudly carried his new bookbag into the first grade class in the Belgian school and hung it on the hook on the side of his desk as the other children did. Imagine his consternation when the teacher came along and took out most of the books! She would keep them for him until the time came to use a particular book, but how was this little American to know that?

Bobby has not one single good memory of that school. The other boys in our hostel all went into second grade; there was no one to interpret for him or speak up for him to his teacher. We were not allowed to visit or to have a conference with the teacher. We lived only 50 miles from the city, but Bobby was not encouraged to visit home on weekends; re-entry became more difficult. When we visited the city, Bobby's schoolbag would be full of papers he had never handed in because he hadn't finished them. Some he did finish later but lacked the courage to give the teacher.

Bobby did come home for his birthday.   That first year we brought all the boys down to Sona Bata to celebrate. The cake I made for the occasion barely rose.

One of the boys exclaimed, "That's a birthday pancake!"

Somehow Bobby survived the year. He did have happy times at the hostel. Sigrid reported that once he said to her, "Aunt Sig, I'm sick."

"Where do you hurt, Bobby?"

"What's that kind of sick? HOMEsick."

The school year ended. What about second grade? Now he knew French. The second year should be much easier. We sent him back. Don and Bunny were hostel parents. I think the whole hostel went swimming to celebrate the week Bobby didn't cry once.

Years later I asked Bunny, "What would you have done with this boy who's having real problems at school and in the hostel?"

She replied, "I'd give him a roommate like Tim." Tim was Bobby's roommate—smart but easygoing, cheerful, a lifelong friend.

Grace had a very scary adventure our first year in the Congo. We took daraprim to prevent malaria. It was a very small pill, easy to swallow, not bitter like most antimalarials. We kept it in a little red pill box. We were supposed to take it once a week, but we would forget, so one day I decided to keep the box on the dining room table to remind us. I should have been warned when three-year-old Grace called it "MY daraprim." One night she vomited off and on all night long. Norm was away. In the morning I discovered the pill box was empty. I asked Tata Kimpiatu, the wonderful head nurse at the hospital, what I should do. Since Grace had vomited thoroughly and seemed all right, there didn't seem to be anything to do, except thank God with a full heart. Friends of ours, missionaries in Thailand, lost a child that way. Why the difference?

We were supposed to take four Kikongo exams during our first two years, or certainly during our first term. We arrived in April of 1956, so it must have been dry season (summer in the States) of 1957 when Madelyn went on furlough. We had had a little over a year to learn the language. Madelyn was directing the homemaking school. This level of homemaking school took girls who had started school late and had now completed second grade but would be nearing marriageable age in another three years. Their three years of homemaking school emphasized cooking, sewing and other needlecraft, cleaning, laundry (most Congolese men ironed their own shirts), and agriculture. They also included rudiments of French, arithmetic, and other general subjects. Madelyn was very good at it. When Madelyn went on furlough,

Eva added that school to the two she was already directing, the regular elementary school and a course for teachers. By Christmas time Eva realized it was too much; someone else had to take the homemaking school. On paper I had the best qualifications; homemaking skills were not among them, but when the second semester started, there I was in Madelyn's office, trying to make sense of my new job.

I enjoyed the course I taught the girls. It was called Conversations. It turned out the subject matter was geography. Instead of starting with their school and town, it began with the universe and worked down. I consulted my encyclopedia since there was no textbook. I told the girls, "There's a star called Betelguese that's so big, if its center were at the center of our sun, the earth would be swallowed up in it."

One girl got the point and asked, "If one star is that big, how big are the heavens?"

A moment for worship.

But now I needed to find out what was going on in all the courses. And what were those little black pellets rolling around in Madelyn's drawer? Oh, papaya seeds. That must have been an extra good papaya and she'd saved the seeds to plant.

I don't remember how much I learned in her office that day, but I'll always remember the second day. The agricultural inspector came. We lived in dread of a surprise visit from a Belgian school inspector. On his report depended the subsidies our schools received, that paid the Congolese teachers' salaries. The inspectors left us free to teach religion as we saw fit, but they did expect us to keep high academic standards. Now here was an inspector. He wanted to see the girls' gardens. I didn't know where the gardens were! Fortunately there was one woman whose job was to supervise the girls' work in their gardens. She showed the inspector around.

The other crisis appeared when one of the three homeroom teachers got sick. Norm diagnosed tuberculosis and decreed that she had to quit teaching until she got better. Also, she was not to carry heavy loads up and down hills. When she was rebuked for toting a five-gallon demijohn of water up from the spring on her head, she protested, "Only one!" Ordinarily women would carry three in a large round dishpan on their head.

The other woman teacher in the homemaking school had seven children. When a new one came along, she brought her to class, where the baby slept in a washtub at the back of the room. When she woke up hungry, Mrs. Tsiebele would nurse her, going on teaching. A real demonstration of practical, indigenous homemaking! But now someone had to take the other teacher's classes until I could find a substitute. Norm eventually lent me his best nursing student! In the meantime I tried to teach all the regular courses—not cooking or sewing; we had special teachers for those. The hardest were agriculture and Kikongo grammar. The homeroom teacher taught agriculture from a book; the Congolese woman, who had never read the book, supervised it in the fields. I never found out whether there was any relationship between the two. Only the teacher had the book.

So I developed the following didactic method: I would read a paragraph from the book and ask the class, "Do you understand?"

"Yes, Mama," they would assure me.

"Then who will explain it to the class?"

Someone would always volunteer, and by the time she finished I would understand what I had read. The subject matter was fruit trees, and I learned that you don't plant orange trees; you graft them on to lemon trees. Now I wonder why we were teaching this to the girls; women grow manioc and corn and peanuts, but it's men who plant trees. Maybe a more experienced teacher would have skipped that chapter.

I was studying Kikongo grammar, but I was studying it in English. The textbook we were using was written by French-speaking Catholics, and they used a slightly different spelling. I was lost. The first day I asked the girls, "What page are you on?"

They told me.

"And what were you doing on this page?"

They told me.

"OK, keep on doing it."

Finally they came to a word I recognized, and it all became clear. They were taking a verb—in this case *sonika,* "to write," and making it into a noun, the doer of the action. I knew *nsoniki,* "writer," as it's the word used for "scribe" in the Bible, and our Kikongo text was strong on Bible passages. (Norm learned medical Kikongo, I learned kitchen Kikongo, and we both learned Bible Kikongo.) Then they added the object and put it in the plural, so we had *nsoniki a minkanda,* "a writer of books." But what could be more absurd than a first-term English-speaking missionary trying to teach Congolese village girls their own language?

The Sona Bata mission station had been founded in 1908, so 1958 marked Sona Bata's fiftieth anniversary, its golden jubilee. Great plans were made for a celebration. "Eva, will you create a play to show the history of Sona Bata?" asked Roland.

"Yes, I will. I'll invite the oldest chiefs over for tea and listen to their memories of the early days." She found three elderly chiefs and laid in a supply of cookies. When the old men were ensconced in her living room with their tea, she emptied a boxful of cookies onto a platter and offered it to the oldest chief. He graciously accepted the whole platter. Fortunately she had two more boxes and two more platters, so each chief could be treated the same. When the conversation was over and it was time to go home, Eva returned each chief's uneaten cookies to their box and sent each one home satisfied and provided with a supply of cookies for the future. She now had lots of ideas for the play, scenes to cover the fifty years. Of course there would be speeches too, and singing.

Station people were not the only ones making plans. During the 50 years, many boys and young men had graduated from the Sona Bata schools, beginning with the most rudimentary education. In recent years girls had graduated too, including the first female Congolese nurses, and of course now there were multiple schools. Most of these grads now lived in Leopoldville, and many of them planned to come to the celebration at Sona Bata. The train made it convenient. They also ordered a steer from the ranch down the line, which they would cook at Sona Bata.

The big day came. Actors were ready in costume for the great history play. Speechmakers, local and old grads, were looking forward to their turns. Of course there were no beds for the horde of old grads, but people were not worrying about that. Then the steer arrived several hours late. It takes time to cook a steer. By the time everyone had eaten, the program began about the time it was scheduled to end. You remember, the generator, in its little house between the two major hills, could run from 6:00 to 9:00 p.m. It was now 9:00. The play began. It had multiple scenes. Roland watched the generator and wondered how long he could stretch its performance without burning it out. Finally, at 11:00, he turned it off. Consternation! Anger! Resentment. Those speeches were never made. Finally people gave up in disgust and in the dark and found some place to sleep. The great day ended with a thud.

In the morning the sun rose on a sorry sight. People had slept in the church and outdoors. All the trash and garbage of the night before littered the space that had been filled with celebrating people. When our good doctor saw the situation, he started cleaning up. After a while another man joined him, one of those from the city. I hope there were several others who helped in the work. Some time later, one of the local men asked Norm, "Do you know that man who was helping you?"

"No," Norm admitted. "Who is he?"

"That's Kasavubu."

Mr. Kasavubu was the head of ABAKO, the political party of the Bakongo, the large tribe that inhabited our part of the Congo. Educated in Catholic schools, he had become Protestant. He had held various jobs, including work for the colonial government. He had begun striving for independence while still holding the government job. At first he had gone along with the Belgians' 30-year-plan, but as the party grew stronger he insisted on an earlier date. He was not a Sona Bata graduate, but of course it was important for him to be part of this large gathering of Bakongo at the 50-year-old station of Sona Bata. He made no speech; he just quietly joined in the grungy cleanup work.

January 4, 1959, Kasavubu was to speak at the enormous stadium in Leopoldville. Passion for independence had grown. The crowd pushing its way into the stadium was immense. Police tried to regulate the flow. The temper of the people was such, and there were so many of them, that they were not about to tolerate any constraint. There was also conflict between political parties. Because it represented the large area from Leopoldville to the coast, and because it had been the most active in the struggle for independence, ABAKO was the dominant party, but of course people from all over the country came to the capital, and every large tribe had its own party. A riot broke out; some people were killed. The Congolese named January 4 the Day of the Martyrs, calling those who were killed martyrs for the cause of independence. Kasavubu did not get to speak, but he was imprisoned as having caused the riot. Two months later he was restored to freedom.

CHAPTER FIVE

Moanza

Flash back to the pioneer days of missions in the Congo. Mpambu was a dedicated young pastor from the other side of the Congo River. He started out on foot with two American missionaries to establish a mission station many miles away on the Inzia River, leaving behind his new bride. He became separated from the other men and ended up walking without them the last eight days to Moanza to share the gospel with people who had never heard it. He was a Mukongo. His dominant tribe populated the large area that extended from the seacoast to Leopoldville, the capital city, also south into Angola, where San Salvador was the capital of the old Kongo kingdom, and north into what was then French Equatorial Africa. Of course this was the first tribe to have contact with Europeans and to receive missionaries, evangelization, literacy.

Trekking east and north, Mpambu was leaving family, clan, tribe, friends, language, and culture. The Basuku, who included Moanza in their territory, were still untouched by any Christian influence. Like other tribes, they believed in *Nzambi-Mpungu,* "God Almighty," but they thought he had created the world and then gone fishing, leaving humans at the mercy of spirits, mostly evil, who had to be propitiated. Illness, accidents, and death were always caused by other people, usually family members. Life was ruled by fear. These beliefs were not strange to Mpambu. He knew what he and others of his tribe had been delivered from. He wanted the Basuku to be delivered too.

The Basuku spoke a different language from the Bakongo, but it was close enough so Mpambu could understand some things, and they could understand some of what he said. In fact, as he approached one village the first man who spotted him spoke loudly enough so Mpambu heard, "Here comes our meat. Let's eat him." Mpambu prayed and by God's grace, the villagers did not act on that idea. In fact, the village chief sent some men with him till he arrived at Moanza, where the other missionaries must have rejoiced to see him.

The Americans stayed three months, working with the local people to construct the first buildings of the mission station. A few people followed their teachings and were baptized. Then the two men left and Mpambu was on his own. His wife joined him and was baptized at Moanza. The couple worked hard, earning money by farming to start a school, teaching young people to read and to follow Jesus. As soon as the boys could read a little they were sent back to their villages to teach others. Four years after his arrival at Moanza, Mpambu reaped the first fruits of his labor, baptizing four men and one woman, and the church at Moanza was born. Seven years later a missionary named Hill joined him. Moanza people used to talk about *Nzambi a Tata Hilu*—Mr. Hill's God.

After his wife's death Mpambu married a Musuku. Few frontier missionaries go that far! By the time we got there Mpambu had died, and his widow had married a Mumbala. What? Another tribe? Yes, some Basuku must have reached into the tribe to the north, and they were now represented at Moanza too. I thought of this strong Christian woman as a bridge between tribes. It's hard being a bridge; you get walked on.

58

Now, in 1959, the senior missionaries at Moanza were Marguerite (Miggs) and a couple we called Ted and Pete. Pete's real name was Matilda; she was very feminine. Cliff and Joy, who'd been in Belgium with us, rounded out the missionary staff. Norm already knew Miggs. While we were at Sona Bata he had been asked to diagnose her by radio. She had an acute attack of something that the Moanza missionary nurse described and Norm diagnosed as a pulmonary thrombosis. Later on the doctor from Vanga saw her and thought it had been a coronary. She was ordered to return to the States. Norm flew in the helicopter that went to pick her up and brought her to Leopoldville. One of the Moanza missionaries contributed a cake pan at the last minute when it was realized that there was no bedpan. Then Norm flew on to the States with Miggs by Pan Am. There his diagnosis was confirmed. In the few days before he returned to the Congo, Norm visited his alma mater, the University of Rochester Medical School, to meet Dan, an American Baptist missionary candidate. Dan had previously taken seminary work. Now, a full-time med student, he was also pastoring a small church! Getting acquainted with Dan filled Norm with hope and excitement for the day when Dan would arrive in Congo. Those hopes were more than realized.

The Moanza station included a beautiful little church, made of the local pinkish stone, a fine elementary school, and a 40-bed hospital, run by a missionary nurse with local staff. Now Moanza was to have a doctor!

All our goods and chattels in the Sona Bata truck, with a Congolese driver along to bring the truck back, we made the arduous trip from Sona Bata to Moanza. Of course that courageous pastor had done it on foot, with no friends from his tribe to welcome him when he got there. We had three missionary homes welcoming us, and somewhat discombobulated because we arrived a day later than expected. We knew not to expect many gas stations along the way, so we had brought

Moanza's beautiful church — building and people!

two extra barrels. When we ran out of gas the men simply went to the back of the trunk to open a barrel. Oh-oh! *"Tala, Tata. Mpamba."*

"What did he say, honey?"

"The barrel sprang a leak. It's empty."

"What do we do now?"

"There's another barrel."

Graduation at the elementary school

"Oh, good."

"Oh-oh! It's our water supply."

Norm turned to the driver, "Tata Diyenga."

"Eyu." (Here I am)

Then Norm told Diyenga in Kikongo, "Take the bicycle to the nearest Catholic mission station. Buy 20 liters of gasoline; don't settle for less."

It was a long wait. Night came on; the children and I curled up in the cab; the men slept under or beside the truck. Finally Diyenga returned, pushing the bicycle with its load of fuel. The first mission station had had only 10 liters of gasoline, so he had obeyed instructions and gone on to the next, almost to Moanza. There he had bought 20 liters and strapped it to the luggage carrier. It proved to be too heavy and broke the carrier. So Diyenga fastened the fuel on in some way and pushed the bike back. We had sometimes criticized him for doing his own thing instead of what he had been told. This time we wished he had used his own good sense!

I've always thought Moanza was our most beautiful church center. The Inzia flows far below the little plateau where the mission station was built. In the mornings fog fills the valley, like a wide white river. Across the river rise range after range of hills. In the other direction a road goes on up to a village at the top of the hill. Near the river the hills are covered with trees, rising very tall from the riverbank to find the sun. In other places they're all grass, looking velvety green from a distance. If you walk through them you find they're not at all velvety.

The mission station was built around the church, with paths leading to it from the hospital at the upper end, the missionary homes overlooking the valley, the school and houses on both sides. Ted and Pete greeted us warmly, assuring us, "Anything you need and don't have, just tell us, and we'll tell you how to get along without it." Actually they met all our needs. There was no market; there was no store. We ate what people came to the door to sell us, plus what we had brought with us. We had imported a lot of canned goods, including large tins of powdered milk, boxes of raisins and other goodies stored in a small metal barrel or box, oatmeal in cans. It was compressed so that when you opened a two-cup can you got seven cups of raw oatmeal out of it. In the past some missionaries had given each other onions for Christmas—bunches of locally grown shallots, which weren't always available. I tried to have a garden, but I'm no gardener, and it turned out our outdoor man wasn't either. In Congo people plant in *plate-bandes,* "square beds" instead of rows. When the plants came up, the ones near the path did pretty well, but those on the other side of the bed looked very sorry. It had been too much work to throw the water that far. My watermelons did not make it. One year when we went to the coast on vacation, we found watermelons on sale at Matadi. They were such a treat I bought one to take with us and even made watermelon rind pickles at the beach house rather than waste any of that precious fruit.

Moanza folk spoke Kisuku, which had a good deal of resemblance to Kikongo. Also, the older people had learned Kikongo, as the missionaries had decided around 1930 that all our stations should use the same language. People were very happy to have a resident doctor. A doctor from Vanga had been coming four times a year to do surgery, as Norm had done from Sona Bata to Boko.

The hospital had 40 beds. There was no X-ray; there hadn't been at Sona Bata either. Old Tata Kitsangi was the senior nurse—no ball of fire, but a man of integrity. He suffered from asthma, and once while we were there he had such a crisis his wife thought he was a goner and started wailing. He protested, "Louise, please!" He lived another 20 years. A younger nurse had graduated from the four-year course at Kimpese and brought more knowledge. The hospital also had a couple of young men who had been trained at Sona Bata. The rest of the staff had pretty much learned by doing. Norm was a good teacher.

Tata Kitsangi consulting with an expectant mother

One day the local government requested (ordered?) Norm to perform an autopsy in a village we did not know. The body had not been buried very deep or very long, so Norm was able to dissect it and find the poison that had killed the man. He sent a sample to the government lab. He also asked one of the men who had been helping him, "If you were going to poison somebody, what plant would you use?" The man readily showed him a plant, and Norm sent samples of that to the lab too. Yes, it matched the poison found in the body. Norm was not required to identify the poisoner.

Sometimes when a patient died at the hospital, Norm wanted to perform an autopsy to make sure of the cause of death. The family had to be convinced to give permission, and convincing them was rarely possible. We were surprised to find that here in the States the family may try to have an autopsy done and find it difficult and very expensive.

Down in Leopoldville, Chet had become the mission secretary. His wife, Margaret, saw that teachers needed help with their religion lessons. All they had was a curriculum that gave them a topic and a Scripture reference for each lesson. So Margaret went over the excellent American Baptist Sunday School materials used in the States, picking out lessons that could be adapted for use in the Congo. For each of the six grades she asked one teacher, "Will you adapt each lesson to your children's needs, teach it, and then write it in Kikongo?"

"Yes, Margaret," I replied. "I'll tackle sixth grade. Sounds interesting."

What a lot of mistakes I made! I started out the first lesson jumping into the story, as it was written in English. "Timoteo didn't even hear his mother calling him that morning." You don't do that in the Congo. You give the title and carefully set the scene before you go into the action.

If I didn't know a word and couldn't find it in our Kikongo dictionary I would look for it in the Bible. This is dangerous, especially in the Old Testament, where scholars don't agree on how to translate some verses. It seems to me there was one word that might mean "orgies" or perhaps "little hills".

There was one girl in my class who was persecuted by the other kids because she was from a different tribe. For one lesson I used the book of Philemon, putting her name in place of Onesimus. I don't know whether it helped or not.

I remember asking the students, "What is the hardest thing you do? Chopping wood, digging gardens, what?" I submitted that forgiving was the hardest. Another time I asked them, "What is the work of a pastor?" and was disappointed to get the answer, "Raising money and building church buildings."

One unit started with Acts and went through the history of the early church. When we got to Revelation, I explained that some scholars thought it had been written by the John who wrote the gospel and the epistles, and others thought it must have been some other John. Someone suggested that it might have been John the Baptist.

I reminded them, "Remember? He had his head chopped off by Herod. Could he have written Revelation after that?"

"We don't know," they replied. "Could he?" It makes a difference when you believe in the living dead!

The missionaries got together for a special meal on Thanksgiving, Christmas, New Year's, and Easter. Since we were four households, we each had a turn at hosting the others. When my turn came, we were to have a goat leg. I thought one leg might not be enough, so I was given two. When it came time to eat, the precious goat legs were not done. *Kiadi!* (sorrow). Also *nsoni!* (shame).

Another time we were having company and had hired an extra boy to help in the kitchen. I went out and found him washing the ice cubes in hot soapy water.

At Moanza we met driver ants, also called army ants. They bivouac and then invade houses in armies, eating everything animal. They don't cross kerosene, so once I supposed I could keep them from going into the dining room by pouring kerosene on the threshold. They simply crawled up the wall and went in higher up. You can dip a little palm frond broom in kerosene, set fire to it, and go along their ranks, burning them up as you go, or you can vacate your house for a day and come back to find it thoroughly rid of cockroaches and all other small pests. The ants travel in columns, with larger ants at intervals along the sides, apparently keeping them in order. Once George and I noticed a small detachment composed of only the larger ants. "An ROTC unit!" he exclaimed.

Bobby had started second grade in the Belgian school in Leopoldville. We brought him home for his birthday in December. Because the country, especially the capital city, was in something of a ferment leading to independence, many Belgians had already left. We did not send Bobby back. What a relief for him! He jumped right into Calvert School in English with his friend Tim. You remember he had done first grade at home and then first grade in French the following year. Now he was plunged into the middle of third grade in English. At first he literally couldn't spell "the," but he was a good sport and caught up fast. One day he was relaxing in the bathtub and informed me, "Mom, I'm a dreamer. You know what a dreamer is?"

"What's a dreamer, Bobby?"

"A dreamer is somebody who's supposed to be doing his work, and he gets to looking at something and thinking all about it, how it's made and everything, and all of a sudden the teacher shouts, 'Abell! *Tu dors?*' [Are you asleep?]"

Grace went to the local school. She told us one day that she knew seven languages. She was right about English. She felt she knew French because in school she had learned to close the door in four tenses. She had learned Kikongo at Sona Bata, playing with other children. Here boys played with boys and girls with girls, and spoke Kisuku, so she was learning that. The other tribe represented at Moanza was the Bambala, who spoke Kimbala. *Mbala* happens to be the word for "sweet potato," so when Grace first heard about Kimbala she exclaimed in delight, "The language of sweet potatoes!" The other two languages? Someone had taught her a phrase in Chinese, which she thought was Japanese, so she counted that as one of her languages. And the seventh was pig latin.

At Moanza, girls played with girls

I was assigned the job of preparing the annual Christmas pageant. I hoped the people from the village up on the hill would come down for it, so I wanted it to be in Kisuku. "All right," my committee agreed, "but when government people (Roman officials in the play) speak they have to use Kikongo *de l'État* (government Kikongo, the trade language also known as Kituba)."

Instead of trying to change scenes on the platform in church, we had the audience move from one scene to another along the road. The first little temporary house built for the performance showed a Christian family on Christmas Day, visited by a little girl from a non-Christian family. That gave the father an opportunity to open the Bible and start telling the Christmas story. The audience moved to the next *fokola* (temporary shelter), where the angel visited Mary and from which she started off to see Elizabeth. In the third *fokola* Joseph and Mary were gazing in awe at their newborn baby. Behind the church and the road we were following was an open space that served as a soccer field.

This day it was a field where shepherds were keeping watch over their sheep—real sheep, one per shepherd. After they visited Bethlehem and saw Jesus, we ended up at the church, where Simeon welcomed the Messiah, blessed and warned his parents. At Moanza several old men had lost their sight from river blindness. We chose one of those men for Simeon. He was reduced to making balls of string for a living, but his faith was still strong.

In 1960 *Mbundani,* the annual Convention of Baptist Churches of Western Congo, was to meet at Moanza, and we missionary women, under the capable direction of Pete, had the responsibility of preparing meals for 54 people. I remember finding out how an avocado from the tree near our house dressed up a green salad very nicely. Now I wonder how many of the Congolese appreciated raw vegetables. I was responsible for the squash for one meal. I discovered that 54 people do

Visiting Bethlehem, they saw Jesus! I loved directing the Christmas pageant

not eat nine times as much squash as six people. That might be because Congolese are used to eating the seeds, not the flesh.

Pete was concerned about Joy working too hard because she was pregnant. Unfortunately I let it slip that we were expecting a third child also. In due course Norm delivered Linda, a breech baby but just fine. Linda and Marjorie were to become great friends.

Independence was coming! Out here in the boondocks few people had any idea what it meant. It was something wonderful, but what? Con artists sold boxes of dirt, which they assured people would turn to gold when independence came. Tim's friends teased him: "We're going to get our independence, and you're not going to get any."

One loyal pal assured him, "When I get my independence, I'll give you some."

Sometime during that Moanza year we made a trip to Leopoldville. The Bontragers found us one evening where we were staying at the Mission Guest House. They were Leopoldville missionaries, in charge of the Protestant printing press. They asked Norm if he would go with them to visit a patient. Of course he agreed. Where they took him in the city I don't know, but the patient turned out to be Mr. Kasavubu. Norm examined him and told him, "You need medical attention. You should be in a hospital."

"Not in the city," decreed the politician. "The Belgians would find me right away."

"Then go to IME," Norm suggested.

"No, I need to be close enough to keep my finger on things. I'll go to Sona Bata."

The hospital at Sona Bata was now the responsibility of a recently married woman doctor. Norm wanted to spare her the responsibility of treating, and housing, the head of ABAKO, but he was not able to influence Kasavubu to change his decision. The hospital had no private rooms, and no one was about to put Mr. Kasavubu in a ward. The doctor was, naturally, occupying the doctor's house, where we had lived for the previous three years. Kasavubu was given the children's veranda bedroom. So yes, Grace, Kasavubu did stay in your room—but not while it was yours. It must have been difficult to keep his whereabouts a secret, since an armed guard was always on duty outside his room—supplied by Kasavubu or ABAKO, not by the hospital!

We were scheduled for furlough. Frank, a physician, and his wife, Joan, were to replace us. In fact, they came a month before we left, giving time for an orderly transfer of the work. We moved out of our house so they could move in. I provided three boxes for Bobby and Grace to sort their stuff into:

The hospital staff during the transition of supervision from Norm to Frank

Take to the States. Store here. Give away. When I checked on their progress, almost everything was in the first box and nothing in the third.

There was a small guest house just down the hill from our house; we occupied that. It was so hot in that bunk bed at afternoon siesta time, and Marjorie was getting bigger and heavier. When the time came to leave, we had a sale, displaying things in the living room of the little guest house and inviting people in to buy at rock bottom prices. Foolishly I had included gift wrapping paper, and when everyone had left we discovered some had secreted things in the paper and had got even more for their money than we had planned. We had got rid of not only everything we had for sale but also the cushions from the guest house chairs.

Our departure was set for June 24. We would miss Congo's Independence Day by less than a week. Kasavubu was elected the first president of the newly independent country. He would serve five years, during a succession of prime ministers. When Kasavubu was no longer in office, he retired to his natal region, a good deal downriver from our area. There he died. A rumor circulated that he had been poisoned. It's not impossible, but that kind of rumor was very common, and Dr. Abell knew that Mr. Kasavubu had suffered for years from enough medical problems to take his life without any human assistance.

CHAPTER SIX

Watermelon

We had sailed from New York to Europe and again from Belgium to the Congo, but by 1960 it had become more economical to fly. My parents were in New York City to meet the Pan Am plane and were duly impressed by my rounded appearance. Mother called it my watermelon. Not realizing how very well one was fed on transatlantic flights, they took us to an expensive restaurant in the terminal. I remember being served 7-Up in an elegant glass surrounded by crushed ice.

On June 30 the Congo became an independent country. We scanned the New York Times for news. There wasn't any. Never has it been so apparent to us that no news is good news. Finally on July 7 the news broke, and it was not good.

Way back in the bush people had no idea what independence meant. In the capital and the area between it and the coast where our down-country stations (those between Leopoldville and the mouth of the river) were located, expectations rose high. Not only would all the government officials be Congolese; of course all the Belgian army officers would be replaced by Congolese; and furthermore, Congolese would get the Belgians' houses and wives.

Congolese did take over all the government posts. In many cases the man who had been a clerk in the territorial administrator's office succeeded to the main desk. No one else knew as much about the job. Many Belgians did leave, and of course some houses must have changed hands. Wives did not. And the Belgian army officers were not immediately replaced, nor did the soldiers become richer. Having guns, some decided to take matters into their own hands. This happened at one army camp near our Nsona Mpangu station; our missionaries were attacked, beaten and mistreated. There was a general evacuation of white people, whether Belgian, American, or Portuguese, as many storekeepers were. Frank, the doctor, never did go back to Moanza. The New York Times gave fragmentary accounts. One small item reported that a helicopter landed at Kimpese to pick up missionaries but didn't find any. There was never any follow-up in the paper, and we wanted to know. It turned out that a different helicopter had arrived there first and evacuated the folk in question.

At Sona Bata, nurse Kimpiatu, who had assisted Norm in surgery, took over the leadership of the hospital, doing minor surgery and emergencies (Caesarean sections and hernias), and reported later that he had not lost a single surgery patient.

In the States, we were planning to spend our furlough in one of the two houses in the Boston area that our mission board kept for that purpose. We were to live in Judson House in Malden, a large house built in 1742 where Adoniram Judson, the first American Baptist foreign missionary, was born.

However, we stayed with my parents, the Brokaws, in New Hartford, New York, until mid-August. The baby was due in September. When the time came to travel, for once we were all ready the night before, with suitcases packed and in or on the Brokaws' car. Norm had been in New York City and came back that night after I'd gone to bed. He felt my abdomen and informed me that I was in labor. So the next morning, instead of heading for Massachusetts, we unstrapped my suitcase from the top of the car and went to see a doctor.

After examining me, he pronounced, "Well, you may have been in labor, but you're not in labor now."

"Should we go to Boston today?"

"I can't tell you that."

We decided to go ahead and arrived safely in Malden. Judson House was divided into two apartments. At the moment the widow of a Baptist minister was living downstairs, taking care of the house until missionaries came. She welcomed us but, not surprisingly, could not recommend an obstetrician in Malden. She handed us a phone book and we went to the yellow pages. August is a good month for vacations. We went down the list alphabetically and finally contacted Dr. Wilder. Since my watermelon was quiet, we made an appointment for the next morning.

"You're not in labor now, but it could happen any time."

Mother stayed. After a week or so Dad went back to his church.

We moved into the upstairs apartment and waited for the baby. Bobby and Grace started school. Every night I had false labor. Every night it went on for a while and then stopped. I became impossible to live with. Mother finally went home.

Early one September morning it was the real thing. Norm woke the kids up and took them to the hospital with us, where they stayed in the waiting room. The doctor came. The nurses prepped me, and everybody waited for the moment to take me to the delivery room. Finally Norm had to take Bobby and Grace to school; the doctor popped home for breakfast. That was when Marjorie decided to make her appearance.

Because of a diarrhea scare in the nursery, they were taking a throat swab on all mothers. They found staph aureus in my throat, although I had no symptoms, so I was not allowed to have Marjorie with me.

Since I wanted to nurse her, and Mother had returned to help, they let me take her home at two days.

So a very young Marjorie went to live in the house where Adoniram Judson had preceded her by some 150 years. In her room there was a crib that surely did not date back to Adoniram's birth but wasn't very up-to-date either. The side did not go up and down but stayed at a perennial mid-height. When Marjorie grew able to pull herself up, she could easily fall out, and did. At first all I could think of to do was put a folded blanket on the floor to cushion her fall.

Soon a couple from Burma came to the downstairs apartment. Ed was very ill; they had been unable to treat him in Burma and expected him to die. He and his wife wanted to try the Lahey Clinic in Boston. Lo and behold, the obstruction in his stomach was caused by a knot of whipworms. Once they were removed he was able to eat again and quickly gained strength. Judson House was full of praise to God!

One day Bobby came home with a friend from school. The other boy asked, "Do you have any sisters?"

Bobby replied, "Yes, this is one of them," indicating Grace. It was a new thought to me that now he had two sisters.

Norm sharpened his skills by observing in the Surgery Department of Massachusetts General Hospital. He attended grand rounds and operations, refreshed his memory on things a bush doctor might forget, and acquired new knowledge that hadn't been available when he went to med school and did his residency.

We attended First Baptist Church in Malden and had opportunities to speak in the black Baptist church as well. On the way we would pass a Catholic store that had figurines of Mary and others in the window.

Grace, seven, called it the *biteki* store. *Biteki* is the Kikongo word for idols, also dolls. I used to attend the women's meetings. One month the subject of the meeting was dollhouses. When I spoke to the group the following month, my talk was entitled "Trivia." Do we really want to devote our precious time together as Christian women to talk about dollhouses and such?

In January Don and Betsy with their four children came to live in the downstairs apartment. They had been at Nsona Mpangu when it was attacked. When they were new in Congo Norm had delivered Tonda, who was now two years old.

In July of 1960 there were no Congolese doctors who had been trained in the Congo. The first class graduated from the medical school later that year. There were some 750 expatriate doctors for a country of 22,000,000 people. After the massive evacuation 250 were left. Norm was impatient to get back. The mission board now planned to send him and Don back together. Betsy and I would hold the fort at Judson House until the school year ended, when we'd be allowed to rejoin our husbands on the field.

At the last minute the board changed their minds. They decided Betsy had suffered enough that she should not be deprived of her husband. They must have been divinely guided. Norm went off in January 1961 without Don. He lived with Wes at Moanza, in Ted and Pete's house. It was an emotional moment when Norm walked into their dining room and saw Pete's sweater over the back of the chair where she always put it. Later he found the Moanza people had also kept the drinking water she had had boiled before they were evacuated.

CHAPTER SEVEN

Five Months Is Too Long

Norm had plenty to do to keep him busy. Frank was sent to the 100-bed hospital at Vanga to replace the experienced doctor, who had already retired once or twice and come back because he was needed. He would not return again after evacuation. He was a competent, rapid surgeon. Besides supervising all the medical work, he took care of administration and finances. Now these fell into the laps of the Congolese staff, nurses and less trained people. With the heady ferment of independence, they were glad to have the responsibility for what only the white man had done before. When Frank arrived, they saw no reason to share administration and finances with him. He could do surgery. They were very surprised to find that the new doctor was not willing to stay under those circumstances. He was sent to IME, the big union hospital at Kimpese, where he eventually became director.

Now Vanga lacked a doctor and was added to the hospitals Norm needed to visit. He was in charge of the small hospital at Moanza, where he lived, but he couldn't spend much time there because he needed to visit other institutions, both mission and government, that had lost their doctors.

As the months went by, the Vanga staff learned that administration and finances could become quite difficult; also, a doctor sent to take charge of a hospital will expect to have some say in administration and finances. This prepared the ground so that when Norm visited Vanga he was able to have serious talks with the staff and prepare the way for the new missionary, Dr. Dan, who would expand the Vanga hospital's ministry and reputation beyond anyone's dreams, except perhaps his.

At Moanza Norm had a portable reel-to-reel tape recorder, which he sometimes used to send me messages. Early one morning he was out walking around with the recorder hanging from his shoulder, recording for me. He told me, "Yesterday was payday at the hospital, but there wasn't enough money in the box to pay everybody." Since he was moving as he spoke, his voice came out quavery.

George was taking graduate work at Harvard and came to see us from time to time. He predicted, "If you play that tape in the churches, people will immediately reach into their pockets and shell out so the box will have enough money next month." Alas, I didn't take the tape to churches. It wouldn't have been a good solution to the problem—it was an example of what Norm called "aid dropped by parachute" in contrast to a long-term solution such as more patients, better bill collection, perhaps moving a staff person to a different position, such as a rural dispensary. But it would have been fun to see if folk would respond to that quavery voice telling the sad news.

One thing Norm talked about was Wes' adventures. Wes was an outstanding missionary who cared greatly for his Congolese brothers and didn't shrink from taking chances. Once he was driving people somewhere in a truck when a group of soldiers flagged them down peremptorily. Oh-oh, what now? It turned out they needed him to take a woman in labor to the hospital.

Another time Wes had a group of students in the truck when they were stopped at a checkpoint. Some of the students didn't have all the identification papers they needed, so they were hauled off to jail. "If they're going, I'm going too," Wes informed the soldiers. Accordingly he spent the night in jail with the students—and the bedbugs, no doubt.

Recounting this, Norm complained, "Nothing ever happens to me!"

Well, one Sunday something did happen. Mission Aviation Fellowship had not worked in the Belgian Congo. Norm had to make all those trips to other hospitals by truck. But after independence MAF did start flying there. Norm was commissioned to find a good site for an airstrip at Moanza—not an easy assignment, if you remember that the terrain there is hills and more hills. He had been scouting around and found a possible site, and men had started clearing it. Officials at the nearest government post got wind of this, and one Sunday during church a truckload of them drove into the station demanding of the Moanza people, "Turn your doctor over to us!" They were afraid the airstrip would be used for landing paratroopers!

Worshiping in church, Norm knew nothing of this until the service was over and he came out, to find the government truck surrounded by men with machetes, not about to surrender their doctor! He was able to reassure the officials, "No paratroopers will land here. The strip will be long enough for only very small planes."

After several months Norm developed tendonitis, an inflammation of the rotator cuff which gave him shoulder pain. He had no doubt used his arm unwisely. Also, he'd been separated from his wife and children too long. What do families do when one is in the military?

At Judson House, Don was off on deputation. Their little Becky had been unwell for some time, and Betsy took her to the doctor. The diagnosis: leukemia. Don came home as fast as he could. Good thing he wasn't in the Congo. There followed many medical visits and lots of talk about the Jimmy Fund, set up to combat leukemia and pay for its costs. Becky was a charming three-year-old; they said, "Her picture will make lots of money for the Jimmy Fund," but when a camera appeared Becky's smiles went into hiding.

In those days there wasn't enough that could be done for leukemia. As her parents put it, "It took two years watching her suffer before we were willing to let her go."

June came; the kids were out of school. They had been given the opportunity to set up little savings accounts. With her savings Grace went to the store and proudly bought her own Cinderella watch.

We were to fly to Congo July 4. I busily bought our refit, items we would need for the next term, the term Norm had already started. There were shoes for the children in several sizes for the next few years. I replaced some of the tableware we had taken out the first time. When we first left the States aluminum tumblers in different colors were in style, but when we offered one to a senior missionary at Moanza she stated, "I don't drink out of a tin cup." I searched for a glass tumbler and tried again. She added, "Or a jelly glass." So now I bought proper glass glasses. We never left anything in the store packing; we always took it out and protected it between cloth items we were taking anyway, to save space. I think I lost one of those pretty little jelly glasses that way on the first experience. That was the only breakage. But for a later term we lined a metal barrel with a 2-inch foam mattress and then filled the interior with miscellaneous household items, including a bottle of vanilla, which managed to break, adding unusual color and temporary fragrance to several other things.

My parents came again to help me with the packing. It would have been good to send the things off a month or so before we left, but we were never that foresighted. The transport people must have come for them July 3rd, and the Fourth of July we were on our way for our second term.

CHAPTER EIGHT

A Multicolored Cloth

Our plane duly arrived in Leopoldville and we were met by a very happy husband and daddy. We stayed in the capital city a little while. During that time we took a trip to Nsona Mpangu, the station where Don and Betsy had been. Their house had been left exactly the way it was when they evacuated. On the way we stopped at our first station, Sona Bata, glad to see old friends. One was a young male nurse who had married his sweet Catholic bride during our time there. When their first baby came, she had to be delivered by Caesarean section. The father was so grateful for the good outcome for mother and child that they named the baby Abelline. That was flattering, but less so when we discovered the child's other name: *Mpesi*. That means "cockroach." We asked, "Why would you name a child Cockroach?"

We were told, "A cockroach eats everything. We want to be sure this child will always have enough to eat." But if we'd asked someone else we might have got a different answer. On this visit we posed for a photo, Abelline's mother holding Marjorie and I holding Abelline. Many years later we found Abelline working as an auxiliary nurse at IME.

Jean with Abelline, her mother with Marjorie

Bobby and Grace had stayed with friends in the city. The children were taken to a swimming pool, where Grace took off her prized watch at the last minute and laid it carefully on the bench in the changing room. When she came back after swimming, the watch was gone. *Kiadi!* (sorrow). Grace learned early to weather disappointments.

It was August by the time we actually made it back to Moanza. And our beloved colleagues Cliff and Joy didn't get there till September. The mission board decreed Norm should not leave Moanza before the other missionary family came. He was happy with the decision, as he needed time to work at his own hospital, but what was the board thinking, he shouldn't leave his family "alone"? Didn't they count our Congolese "family," who surely would have protected us if any protecting was needed?

When both families were back, the pastor held a special welcoming service for us in church. This is the way he put it: "You know, in our country the women wear cloths of different, bright colors, but we men wear plain khaki shirts. For a while we were like a khaki shirt, all the same color, but now that our white friends are back we're like a multicolored cloth."

It was good to be back. We lived in the house on the other end of missionary row this time, the one Miggs had occupied. Neither she nor Ted and Pete would be coming back; they were about ready for retirement anyway. Cliff and Joy had the big house that had been Ted and Pete's, where Wes and Norm had led their bachelor existence for five months.

At the beginning of our furlough we had talked about speaking French one meal a day and Kikongo one meal. That lasted about one day. Now Bobby went out and played with his friends and soon got his language proficiency back. Grace's friends didn't come so often; girls had to help their mothers and were free only on Sundays. And when they did appear she hid behind a curtain because she'd forgotten how to talk with them!

Grace had promised, "I'll take all the care of the baby!" She had turned eight in the States and was indeed a great help. We celebrated Marjorie's first birthday in September. She sat happily in a playpen, enjoying the gift wrap more than the presents.

Remember the stuff we had shipped just before we left the States July 4? It arrived in the port of Matadi, made it through customs all right, must have been put on a train to Leopoldville, then a boat up the Congo River, branching off into the Kwa, then the Kasai. At Mbandaka, where the Kwilu runs into the Kasai, it was transshipped to a smaller boat to ascend the Kwilu and eventually the beautiful little Inzia River on which or above which Moanza was built. The trouble was that by this time it was October and rainy season had begun. Our barrels and cases came safely off the boat into the little warehouse on the bank, but the road from there to the church center stayed so muddy the truck couldn't make the trip down to get our freight. The barrels and cases stayed in the warehouse.

One day toward the end of October 1961, a boy was brought in to the hospital who had fallen from a tree and been impaled on a broken branch on the way down. His intestine was pierced; Norm had to perform a colostomy to let the intestine heal.

A previous surgical challenge had involved a man whose gun had accidentally gone off while standing vertical between his knees and shot off his jaw. Norm needed a nasogastric tube so the man could be fed, but there wasn't any available. He tried another kind of tube. It was too small; it just curled up and never made it down to the stomach. That man had to be flown to Vanga. Thank God for MAF!

But now, operating on the boy, Norm wasn't feeling too well himself. He stayed in bed the next day, saying, "I guess I've got malaria"—a pretty likely diagnosis in the tropics.

"It seems more like flu to me," I judged, and so did a doctor who happened to visit Moanza in the ensuing days. Whatever it was, it wasn't getting better.

The time came to undo the boy's colostomy. Norm didn't have the strength to go up to the hospital, so they brought the boy to our house and laid him on sterile sheets on our living room floor. Norm knelt beside him and did the necessary surgery. When his strength ran out he would lie on his side and rest until he could get back to work. Grace remembers coming into the adjoining dining room and seeing the strange sight of her dad on his side and other members of the surgical team kneeling around someone lying in the middle of the living room floor. I hadn't thought to inform the kids of what was going on! Grace says, "I decided I wasn't supposed to be there."

It may have been the next day that Norm noticed weakness in his left hand and arm. Neither malaria nor flu would explain that. We got on the radio and asked a doctor in Leopoldville, "Could you come up on the next plane?"

He suggested, "Why don't you fly down to Leopoldville instead?" MAF pilot John and his wife had planned a little visit to Moanza. I had made a mango cake in preparation for their coming. Now we had to ask them instead of visiting us to take us to the city.

Joy offered to keep Bobby and Grace while we were away. The children had been together in school, one mother teaching Tim and our Bobby in the same grade and the other one taking our Grace and Rick, a year apart. Now Joy would have all the teaching to do, plus mothering. Little Marjorie, 13 months old, and I got on the plane with Norm, who lay on a mattress on the floor. "Can you walk?" the pilot had asked him.

"No," Norm admitted. Then he amended, "Well, I could walk a few steps." John didn't ask him to.

Some time later I saw the diary Grace was keeping at that time. The day after our departure she wrote, "They did not come back." The next day: "They stil [sic] did not come." The following day: "They stil did not come" and so on, day after day. It made very poignant reading until Grace confessed that it had been one of those times when you don't write in your diary every day and fill in whatever you can remember when you finally try to catch up. You can see what she remembered.

CHAPTER NINE

Unexpected Furlough

We didn't know it at the time, but boarding that little MAF plane to leave Moanza in late 1961 was to signal the end of our truncated second term in Congo, and a new kind of life for Norm. We had been rejoicing that our two missionary families were back at Moanza, resuming our work or starting new work. Now everything was changed again.

What did Norm have? Nobody thought it could be polio. We had all received a full course of Salk vaccine back in 1956. But for whatever reason, Norm's left hand was paralyzed, and he was steadily getting weaker. Someone suggested Guillain-Barré syndrome. It causes paralysis somewhat similar to polio. But it wasn't that.

In Leopoldville Norm was taken to the white hospital. It wasn't necessarily painted white; it was intended for white people, in contrast to the humongous hospital available to Africans—crowded, noisy, dirty, not brimming with hope. This time I did not complain that my husband got better treatment than the Congolese. We wouldn't have thought of taking him to the city hospital even for a relatively minor illness or accident; now he was undiagnosed with something major, mysterious and scary.

The white hospital had lovely big rooms, each with access to the veranda. We learned to our surprise that, just as in the hospitals we served, each patient needed a family member to stay with him—but I did not have to prepare his meals. Little Marjorie was just learning to walk; the stone tile floors, slanted toward the veranda to make mopping easier, didn't help any. Besides, she wasn't welcome. There was even a bed for me (I didn't have to unroll a mat under my husband's bed as a Congolese wife would do!), but no provision for a toddler. Margaret, whose husband, Chet, was mission secretary, graciously offered to care for her most of the time along with all her regular responsibilities. Once during that stay the young people staffing UMH, the interdenominational mission guest house, kept her for me for an afternoon. They introduced her to Coca-Cola!

Norm's paralysis proved to be more extensive than appreciated at first. Only his left arm and hand were completely paralyzed; his legs, back and shoulders had several partially paralyzed muscles and his nerves in general were jumpy. It was hard for him to sleep. Sometimes I took him for wheelchair rides; it seems to me we found out later that wasn't a good idea. The doctor gave him a small ball to squeeze in his paralyzed hand. Norm told me, "That's the index of his incompetence to treat this."

The doctor threatened, "If you're not better by next week, I'm going to send the physical therapist to see you." The therapist came and massaged his limbs. I tried to learn how. The doctor said to me, "Oh, you want to *voler le métier* (steal his profession)"!

Eventually Chet and others decided Norm should go to the States to recover—return to Strong Memorial Hospital in Rochester, NY, where he had trained.

So finally, Grace, Mom did come home, although Daddy didn't. I was ready to go with him, but Chet had a much more practical solution in mind: Jerry, mission treasurer, would go with Norm; I would return to Moanza to pack up our belongings and follow in some three weeks' time. Norm and Jerry left on Thanksgiving Day. Norm's brother David met them at Kennedy airport in New York. He remembers, seeing Norm being carried down the stairway in a wheelchair. "I was shocked to find that he couldn't move any one of his four limbs." David accompanied him on the plane to Rochester and on to Strong Memorial Hospital, at his alma mater. ∞

At Moanza I had plenty to do. Of course there was less to pack because those barrels were still in the warehouse down by the river. On the other hand, we needed some of their contents for the trip home. We had a list of the contents of each barrel, but were the shoes we needed the ones in #1 or #4? The road was still muddy; men carried the barrels we needed on poles on their shoulders the old way, not dependent on technology. It behooved me to figure out exactly which barrels I really had to have. When I did come to the shoes Grace had grown into, that I had ordered from a catalog, lo and behold, they were light blue velvet with rhinestones or sequins. Tim remarked in his admiring nine-year-old way, "Those are real diamonds, aren't they!"

Once during those days it occurred to me that Norm might die. Somehow I had never thought that before. I was crying a little as I walked through the house, and our cook decided I was pretty weak.

Many friends came to say good-by and wish us well. They usually included something like this: "I'm sure you'll come back, but in case you don't, could I buy your bed?"

At the hospital in Leopoldville, Norm had received visits from friends, usually from Sona Bata. Their wishes went, "We're praying with all our hearts that you'll get well and come back to help us."

Marc was different. Marc had graduated from the Sona Bata nursing school about the same time as Kimpiatu. He made an excellent nurse, but he decided to go back to school, hoping to become a doctor. He took the first cycle of secondary school at Nsona Mpangu, downriver from Kimpese, and then moved to Kimpese for the second three years. He had four children when he began this endeavor. He would come to

Marc and family

Sona Bata to work at the hospital during vacations. One year he asked
me to tutor him in history; I was glad to do it. The next year it was
physics. I had never taken physics myself, didn't think I was capable
of understanding it, but I took his book and started working on it. I
found out I had been right; willing as I was, I could not help Marc with
physics. Now Marc came to see Norm in the hospital and simply said,
"We're praying with all our hearts that you'll get well." Over the years
he became Norm's best friend.

The children and I were to fly from Leopoldville December 15.
MAF would come for us December 13, giving us two nights in the city.

We really needed that day: Bobby had only short pants, which would not be at all suitable for arriving in New York State in December.

A problem arose. Before my return from Leopoldville a flu bug had attacked Cliff and Joy's children. Now it was Grace's turn. Then Marjorie came down with it too. While I was tending to one on the small plane, the other tossed her cookies just as we were landing. Marjorie was never very sick, but Grace was.

We were very glad to get settled in a large room at UMH. It even had its own bath. Not all the rooms did in those days. Grace made one trip to the bathroom after another. Then she got so weak I had to carry her to the bathroom, and finally I put a waterproof sheet on the bed and just kept changing her. There was a doctor staying at UMH. He gave me Kaopectate with Neomycin. I don't know what we would have done or how we could ever have gone on that plane without it. As it was, Grace gradually improved, and that evening she was hungry. She wanted an egg. This seems hard to believe now, but the kitchen was next door to our room and I was able to go in and soft-cook an egg for her. Then she wanted another. I prepared it and she ate it. The third egg turned out to be one too many, but she was on the mend.

The next day we did make that flight! On the plane was another doctor, a woman missionary on her way back to the States. She had paregoric. Grace was now strong enough to walk, and walk she did. It seemed as if she spent most of the flight in the tiny room at the tail of the plane, even when the RETURN TO YOUR SEAT sign came on. After every trip, another dose of bitter but blessed paregoric. In the morning breakfast was served. I was busy helping Grace when a very small hand came up to my tray table and helped itself to some of my scrambled eggs. Happily, Marjorie was not feeling sick. How grateful I was to God that he provided people to help us and the healing Grace needed!

When we left Leopoldville the temperature measured 80 degrees. In Syracuse, New York, it was 15. My mother had provided coats and caps and scarves and mittens, but they were with her in the terminal building. Now with jet ways, no problem, but getting down off the plane and walking across that windy tarmac—Bobby, Grace, and I with Marjorie— remains in my memory. I always said I never got warm that whole winter.

We took the girls to the doctor as soon as possible. He was more concerned about Marjorie because she was so young, but she got along fine. Grace was recovering too.

Finally we arrived in Rochester, where Norm was. He did have polio. Although the Salk vaccine did wonders, there were a very few people whom it did not protect completely. Perhaps Norm would have been more ill, even died, if he had not been vaccinated. When he was at Strong, there were only two other polio patients in that large hospital, 17-year- old twins who had not been vaccinated. The March of Dimes paid his hospital expenses, once we realized we needed to contact them. Our American Baptist Foreign Mission Society was taking care of them at first.

I had hoped to be able to stay in the missionary apartment at Colgate- Rochester Divinity School, but this was the middle of the school year and the apartment was occupied. Bill had been our pastor during our four years in Rochester. Now he was on the faculty at Colgate-Rochester. He and his wife took us into their home until a more permanent place could be found. How helpful people were to us, at Moanza, in Leopoldville, in Rochester! I'm sure we never expressed our appreciation, just accepted their help and sacrifice of their own convenience. We spent Christmas with Bill and his wife. Then we were allowed to move into a dorm intended for married students.

Strong Memorial Hospital was a far cry from the white hospital in Leopoldville. There were lots of nurses and therapists, and they all knew what they were doing. Norm received whirlpool baths, massage, and all the other treatments that helped polio patients regain as much use of their muscles as possible. I asked his doctor, "How soon will he be able to come home?"

The doctor replied, "In a couple of weeks." After a couple of weeks, the time had become a couple more weeks. This went on until April. It would be so much better to expect a longer wait and then be pleasantly surprised.

A couple we had never met did us a great favor. They were a mature couple, empty nesters, on their way to mission work in Hong Kong. They were buying a new car to take with them. Instead of trading in their old one, they gave it to us. When I visited Norm at the hospital he made me out a maintenance schedule.

Before we ever went overseas we had attended a Camp Farthest Out with Norm's parents and sister and heard of Agnes Sanford, now called "the Grandmother of the Third Wave." That's the third wave of the Holy Spirit. Back in 1954 we first heard of her remarkable success in healing through prayer. Now Mother Abell sent one of Agnes' books to each of us. Norm received her first teaching book, *The Healing Light*. But Mother knew me well and sent me Agnes' first novel, *Oh, Watchman*. All her novels were teaching books too. I opened the book at 10:30 one night when I went to bed in my lonely little room in Eaton Hall. I closed it at 2:30 a.m. when I'd read the last page. It told the most exciting news I could imagine. The Holy Spirit was doing what I'd always thought he should be doing but I didn't know he was —healing people in body and mind, working miracles! Norm took a little longer to read *The Healing Light*, and later when I read it, it took me quite a while because I felt I should put one chapter into practice before I went on to the next. The first chapter explains that God wants us well; if we pray for healing and it doesn't occur, it doesn't mean God doesn't exist, or that he's not able or willing to heal. It just means we need to learn more about how to pray.

As Norm gained strength and some muscles came back, he was able to move around the hospital some. His grandmother was admitted to the same hospital, and he could visit her. She was concerned that perhaps no one would come when she pushed her button. Norm reassured her, "There's always one nurse who comes."

The next time a nurse came into her room, Grandma addressed her, "My grandson tells me there's always one nurse who comes when you call. Are you that nurse?"

Norm also visited the hospital administrator's office. On our return to the Congo in 1961, we had found Kimpiatu, the head nurse who had been so helpful to us at Sona Bata, had carried on the hospital work magnificently after the missionaries were evacuated, performing emergency surgery. Now Norm was able to arrange for him to come to Strong Memorial Hospital and act like a surgical intern, getting valuable experience in surgery and hospital administration. His very first day in the operating room he got to see Siamese twins separated! He was paid as an orderly. Colgate-Rochester allowed him to room

Kimpiatu in the States

in one of their dormitories. An African-American student befriended him, showed him how to use the laundry, also took him to a Black Muslim meeting. Kimpiatu's verdict: "It's political, not religious." One time we were praying at our house (we had moved into an apartment by then) and at the end Kimpiatu said, "Maybe one day things will be much better in Congo, and we'll remember that we prayed."

He was at our apartment when he saw his first snow. He looked out the window and exclaimed, "It's beautiful!" Then he went outside and picked some up. "It's cold!"

At last came the final week of Norm's hospitalization. His roommate was discharged and left a newspaper behind. Norm picked it up and looked through it. There was no reason for him to read the church notices, but this time he did. Lo and behold, Agnes Sanford was coming to Buffalo for a week-long mission, teaching about healing. Norm felt sure the Holy Spirit had supplied that newspaper and directed him to that page.

Norm was discharged from the hospital, and the next week we drove 70 miles to Buffalo every night to hear Agnes Sanford. At one point she invited each of us to choose a subject to pray about in faith. She cautioned us to begin with a little thing, and I tried, but no little thing came to mind, so I prayed for Norm's healing. It didn't happen, but I didn't stop praying. We also were able to talk with Agnes personally after at least one of the sessions. She invited us to come to her School of Pastoral Care in Whitinsville, MA, where we could learn more about prayer for healing.

Norm's first act when he was released from the hospital was to get a book on how to do things with one hand. I helped him continue the exercises he

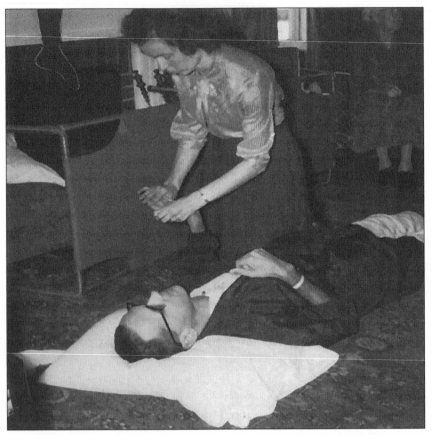

Jean works with Norm's hand

had done in the hospital, and we rejoiced together over any flicker of life in a previously dead muscle. After a while there wasn't any more improvement, but Norm never complained. He just found ways to compensate for the loss of activity in his left arm and hand. I would find just buttoning buttons with one hand terribly frustrating, but he did it for 50 years. Once in a while the top shirt button defied him; he found me a little tool made for overcoming recalcitrant buttons and allowed me to help that much.

In order to get insurance for the car, Norm had to give up his driver's license. It was in driving around Rochester with Norm in the passenger's seat that I really learned city driving.

There was a School of Pastoral Care in May. Norm would have liked me to go, but I didn't see how I could with Bobby and Grace in school, so Norm went. "Was it wonderful, honey?"

"I was blessed, but I felt as if I was on the outside looking in." When I went to the next session in August I determined that wasn't going to happen to me. I told Agnes Sanford about it, and she invited me to a small group that met in an upstairs room during a free time in the morning. I went, and she herself prayed for me to receive the baptism of the Holy Spirit. I was very conscious of the love in the room but didn't feel anything happened at the time of the prayer. I was encouraged to stay alone afterward and be open to speaking in a prayer language. I did for a while, but it didn't occur to me to skip lunch for that purpose! In the years since, I have sometimes used a prayer language but never been sure it was the real thing. But something happened. My roommates at the School saw a change. And when I got home, guess what Norm noticed. I was quieter! I remember taking Bobby to camp and driving home praying away. Good thing there wasn't much traffic.

We were able to attend another School of Pastoral Care together some years later, and since then I've read almost all of Agnes' books. It took a couple of years for *The Healing Light* to find a publisher. Nobody had faith that people would believe it. MacAlaster Park finally took the plunge, and *The Healing Light* met an overwhelming welcome. One day years later, Agnes wasn't feeling well. She told us during her school, "I don't remember what the problem was—sawdust leaking out somewhere." This was very unusual; Agnes could spill hot oil on her arm and just remind it she was protected. But now she was at a low ebb in general. She shared her discouragement with a neighbor on a train, who offered, "I know a book that could help you; it's called *The Healing Light*." Agnes decided that wouldn't meet her need this time. She and two spiritual friends who were in a similar state "made a retreat" at a house in the western desert. First they prayed for healing, but no healing came. Agnes taught us, "When you've prayed for something for several days and nothing happens, ask God how you should pray." She gave us several examples of this. One time she felt that something bad was going to happen in the Pacific Northwest. She asked God if she could pray for it not to happen. He said no.

"Can I pray for it to be less?"

"Yes."

Agnes, in her delightful humility, often said, "My guidance is the most fallible thing there is." If her guidance was fallible, whose in the world is less so?

Another example: Her mother was stricken with Alzheimer's. Agnes asked, "Can I pray for it to be healed?"

"No, she's suffered too much. You can pray for her to remember only the good things."

Agnes did, and her mother quietly lived with only the good memories.

Back to the retreat house in the desert. The three women asked God how they should pray. Each of them separately received the word, "Ask for the Holy Spirit."

Agnes told us, "I thought I had the Holy Spirit." But they prayed two for one, two for one, two for one. Agnes told us, "If a fourth person had been there, he wouldn't have known anything happened. But each of us was conscious, first, that we had been healed of whatever was wrong with us, and second, that we had received power."

After that experience Agnes believed that when one receives water baptism he receives the Holy Spirit, but it's latent. Unless one is expecting to receive the Spirit in his power at that time, it takes another step.

During the summer of 1962 we moved to a half house on Field Street. People were very generous in lending us furniture. Marjorie celebrated her second birthday. One day Grace was washing clothes in the wringer washer in the basement. Marjorie caught the clothes as they came through the wringer. At one point one piece got twisted and

Grace made the wringer go backward briefly. Consternation! Here came Marjorie's fingers through the wringer! Grace did everything right. She hit the right place to loosen the wringer and brought Marjorie upstairs to me. Only then did she start to feel faint.

With the New Year we had passage to return to the Congo by freighter. At one time we were to travel on the *African Lightning*. That didn't seem a very good omen. Our travel was delayed; we finally sailed on the *African Glade*.

During the delay we stayed with my parents. They had a young woman living with them as she continued her education. They had become very fond of her; to some extent she filled the empty spot in their home, with their only child and all her family so far away. Now we met her and were living in the same house. Sadly, I found she rubbed me the wrong way. Was I jealous? I didn't think so, but the enemy got in his licks and robbed me of what the Holy Spirit had given. I was pregnant and not telling anyone but Norm, because you weren't supposed to travel during the first three months. That made me more ornery than I would have been otherwise. It's a period of which I feel very much ashamed. I caused my wonderful mother a lot of suffering.

Eventually we moved to Beacon on the Hudson, where Norm's folks were. One day I took the train to New York City to get a yellow fever shot. On the way back I amused myself by reading the fine print on our tickets. The freighter captain could do anything he wanted to: change the schedule without notice, change the port of call, go backward, even lie on the bottom!

That day I also noticed a small swelling over one hipbone, about the size of a bean. It itched. Norm was as mystified as I was.

On Valentine's Day of 1963 we finally set sail. There were more passengers than on the *Armand Grisard*. Our waiter was very friendly and helpful. "Eddie," I said, "I feel a bit seasick. I'll just have a little fruit, please."

Eddie, experienced with seasick passengers, explained, "Fruit isn't the best idea. Let me bring you some crackers."

He did, and of course he was right. The nausea went away, and we enjoyed the voyage, keeping a monopoly game going in the lounge.

CHAPTER TEN

A New Station

This time we were being sent to Vanga. Norm was supposed to work only half time, so we were going to a station where Dr. Dan was in charge of the medical work. Norm's assignment was the nursing school Dan had already started. Norm enjoyed teaching the students. Of course he wasn't the only teacher. Gini, for instance, taught obstetrics and midwifery. One unit Norm taught was on asepsis and antisepsis. Emphasizing the importance of the skin as a barrier to infection, he quoted an earlier doctor: *"Une piqure d'épingle est une porte ouverte à la mort."* (A pinprick is an open door to death!) Of course he also taught about Louis Pasteur and pasteurization. On the exam one student informed him, *"Le pasteur* (the pastor, rather than Pasteur) *a découvert la méthode de l' épingle pour tuer les microbes."* (discovered the pin method for killing microbes). Norm had visions of a pastor with a large open safety pin, stabbing each microbe as it came along.

We arrived in April; the baby was due in August. Miriam guessed my secret right away, despite my bouffant petticoat. We had left Bobby in the city to stay at the hostel and attend the new American school. Unfortunately the other boys at the hostel were suffering from some malady that had not yet been diagnosed. We were up at Vanga when we heard that it was hepatitis. By the time Bobby came down with it their spring vacation was coming. What to do? We didn't want to bring Bobby to Vanga and expose people there to hepatitis, and the hostel parents didn't really want to spend their vacation at the hostel while all the other children were at home, just to take care of Bobby. So little Marjorie and I went down to the city to take care of Bobby. We got gamma globulin shots and were very careful, washing our hands at every opportunity. By the time spring break was over, Bobby had recovered. The first evening everyone was back, the day before school resumed, we all sat on the floor while Uncle Don showed a move. (That's what the children called him—MKs referred to our missionary colleagues as Uncle or Aunt.) Marjorie felt she had to get up three times during the movie to go wash her hands.

Our first home at Vanga had been a guest house and had apparently grown like Topsy. Going from one room to another, one usually ascended or descended a step. The kitchen was a narrow room along the back of the house, lower than the dining room, and the door from the kitchen to the outside left space between it and the floor. One evening I was at the far end of the long, narrow bathroom and saw something on the floor between me and the door. When the something moved, I realized it was a thin snake. I called Norm; he came and pinned the snake down at the neck with a narrow board. Then he asked me, "Come hold this while I get a machete."

"I'm afraid I won't do it right and he'll get away!"

"Then go get help."

I never would have made a pioneer wife. My admiration for Norma surpasses all bounds. She lived across the (dirt) street in a large house with a basement. Once when she was going downstairs a snake plopped down right in front of her, and she was as scared of snakes as I was. This was her first term. Eventually a nest of snakes was discovered in that basement. I don't think I would have stuck it out. Another snake made its way under the kitchen door before we moved from that house.

At Vanga they spoke Kituba (the trade language based on Kikongo, different from the village Kikongo we had spoken at Sona Bata and Moanza). Kikongo is the name of the language and also the name of the church station where we would eventually live. We proceeded to study Kituba, which is much like Kikongo but with a simplified grammar and influence from Lingala. My recipe file for the cook (this one could read) shows my faltering progress from Kikongo to Kituba. One day I wanted the cook to make angel food cake, so I translated the recipe and called it *Gateau ya Zimbasi* (cake of angels). The next day I wanted a devil's food cake. I called it Chocolate Cake. The most interesting faux pas I'm aware of came when I attempted to translate "Serves eight." I tried to say, "This food will feed eight people." *Dia* means "to eat" in both languages. *Dikila* means "to feed" in Kikongo, so that's what I wrote. Unfortunately I had written in Kituba, "This food will poison eight people."

In July Dr. Dan gave me a prenatal exam. He announced that the baby was still quite small and would surely not be born before the due date in August. It was probably at that time that we showed him the interesting bean sitting over my right pelvic bone. He felt we should have it out posthaste in case it should be malignant. I had not heard of a cancer that itched so did not feel worried. Dan excised the little tumor and then said to Norm, "Well, shall we cut it open?"

Norm mildly replied, "Well, yes." I had supposed that was the whole idea, but Dan was always making deadpan jokes. So they cut it in two and it turned out to be full of a coiled-up little worm—*onchocerca volvulus*. I was lucky, or blessed; if it had been two worms they would have produced lots of eggs and given trouble all over my body. The amazing thing was that this tropical infestation had appeared at least 13 months after we had left the tropics.

Jimmy was born in July. I had intended to go to the hospital for this, my only delivery in the Congo, but there wasn't time. I'd been having false labor every night and had decided that this night I was not going to wake Norm—but I sure wouldn't mind if he woke up himself. And Norm did wake up in time. He examined me and was going to go for Dr. Dan, but I didn't want him to leave me alone, so he went to wake Bobby instead. Bobby, 11, was a sound sleeper, but this time he woke up promptly and did his errand with dispatch. While he was gone, all Dr. Norm could think of to do was boil water! Dr. Dan came, examined me, and directed, "Bobby, go back for nurse Miriam." It is convenient when the doctor's wife is a nurse. In the morning our cook was quite surprised to find a sixth inhabitant in the house.

Jimmy had problems nursing at first, as Bobby had done, but Miriam encouraged me and he succeeded. When he was a month old I wanted to get a picture of him naked; I changed my mind. His poor little bottom looked scalded. I had told the wash jack (laundry man), "Wash the diapers in spring water (carried in pails) because the river water is so polluted." I had also directed him, "Rinse them four times." Now I said, "Wash them in the river." The diaper rash disappeared right away. Congolese, used to washing clothes in a flowing stream, rub each piece thoroughly with bar soap. Of course, in a tub the soap accumulates in the water. Whether or not those diapers had been rinsed four times, a lot of soap had been staying in them. Whatever pollution

Welcoming brand new Jimmy

was in the river, the flowing water washed away the soap. Soon we got a charming picture of a clothed Jimmy in my arms with Norm and the rest of the family admiring him. Grace wrote an excellent story about him for Calvert School, and three-year-old Marjorie considered him her special responsibility. He was the only one of our children to learn colors before the age of three; I figured it was because Marjorie taught him from his stack of nesting rings.

Going back to his earliest infancy, one day I realized that Jimmy didn't startle when someone else came into the room and I spoke to that other person. If my voice was loud enough to carry to the door, it should have been too loud for the baby at my breast. Thunder didn't bother him. I tried clapping my hands over his head; no reaction. I told Doris, "I think my baby's deaf."

"I'll pray for him," she promised. And of course she did. I'll never know whether Jimmy was deaf at first or not, but as he developed he heard just fine. Thank you, Father.

That dry season Scotty and Dolores went on furlough and we moved into their house, all on one level and much roomier. It was the easiest move ever, as the houses were next door to each other and we just moved one room at a time. Our cook made breakfast for us in the old house, moved the kitchen and cooked the noon meal in the new house. He was really fast.

The wash jack was a young fellow. He and Bobby became good friends and even owned a canoe together. When we had lived in the new house for some time, the wash jack came to us and told us, "The cook is stealing things from your kitchen (like dishtowels) and giving them to his mistress." I was more upset about the mistress than the stealing.

We called both men in and talked with them together. After they left Norm told me, "I'm sure from their body language that the wash jack is telling the truth and the cook is guilty as charged." We let him go. I wonder if we could have acted redemptively instead of just dismissing him.

We found Vanga a difficult station. Congolese leaders and missionaries met together for station council. One time several missionaries had gathered in the missionary home where we were meeting; only two Congolese had arrived. One said to the other, "We're the only ones here."

On the other hand, one day one of the missionary women exclaimed, "I can't find Doris anywhere! I've been to every house." Of course she meant every missionary house.

A problem arose that has persisted and grown worse since then. The local people were eager for the school to take in as many students as possible so their children could get diplomas. The missionaries were concerned for the quality of education and pointed out that we didn't have enough teachers to teach all the hours required for the extra sections. We finally asked people to come up from the central office in Leopoldville to mediate. And we prayed that God's will would be done.

The missionaries were outvoted. I suggested that perhaps, even though it didn't seem right to us, the decision was God's will. I did not convince any other missionary. I was to teach French, mornings only. I had to choose whether to teach literature or grammar. I chose literature, hoping to get in some grammar along the way. We had a little library, enriched by a number of paperback books translated from English, not very appropriate for our students. At one time I asked each student in a class to take out a library book, read it, and report on it. I found out that they would read about three pages and then write their report. Some of those students went on to college in the States! How did they do it?

Norm's medical work was more stressful. One senior nurse's aide was especially prickly. At a staff meeting he became quite angry with Norm and, pointing a finger at him (very impolite in the Congo), enunciated with considerable heat, *"Vous êtes capable!"* His intention was clear, but instead of saying, "You are guilty *(coupable),"* he had declared, "You are capable!"

Another time a girl student had written, *"J'ai ceinté par Makalala."* That's execrable French by which she accused a senior nurse of making her pregnant. Talking with the nurse, for some reason Norm unthinkingly handed him the accusation to read, so of course he no longer had any evidence. The girl's reputation didn't lead to unbounded confidence in her anyway. It was at Vanga that Norm developed asthma.

There were some funny experiences. At one time there were two mentally ill people circulating at the church center—a man who would harangue people at the flagpole where the hospital staff gathered every morning, and a woman with a two-year-old boy. One of the missionaries gave her a pair of shorts for the little boy; she somehow managed to get them on herself. The house where we were living had a large veranda; some beds under construction for the nursing students were temporarily housed there. The woman (we started calling her "our lady") decided to take up residence on that veranda. Eventually Norm decided that wasn't a very good idea and moved her to one of the little rooms in the outbuilding behind the house. We found some of the local men were jokingly calling her his concubine!

Once we invited a few of the station leaders to come to our home to pray with us. It was very good. Why didn't we do it regularly?

Norm's dad was a sanitary engineer, and Norm had engineering interests and abilities too. Vanga needed a better water source; Norm decided to prospect for one. He found a good site with a spring down in a valley next to the nursing school. He supervised the construction of a concrete cylinder about six feet in diameter. Wooden forms, inner and outer, were built. Concrete was poured to a depth of three feet, with reinforcing iron. When the concrete was set and ready, the soil was dug out from within and beneath the concrete wall to lower the

Norm's successful engineering project

cylinder to the depth needed to get a good flow of water. A second section of concrete was poured on top of the first, making a six-foot tall cylinder of concrete about three inches thick. Such a heavy structure was not really appropriate for that job, but Norm was not an experienced builder! Anyhow, the work progressed, and sand and clay were removed from under the concrete, letting the cylinder settle. What was not foreseen was the difference in soil on the upstream side (clay) and the downstream side (sand). When the water started coming in faster, it began washing away the sand on the downstream side and it was hard to remove the clay on the other side. The cylinder tipped, impeding any further lowering of the structure. But that did not prevent the good flow of water, and the water source was a success, although Norm was not proud of his Leaning Tower of Vanga. A visiting builder from the States took on the job of piping the water to a reservoir uphill from the hospital.

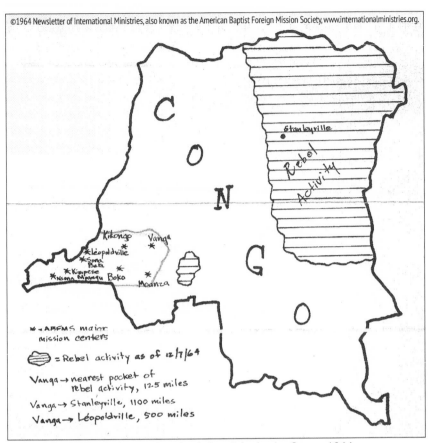

American Baptist mission work and rebel activity in the Congo, 1964

In 1964 Mulele started a rebellion in Bandundu Province, where Vanga was located, but east of us, on the other side of the Kwilu River. This was the precursor of the Simba Rebellion in the northeast part of the country. The rebels felt that the educated people were oppressing them, so they were out to get anyone with an education. A few missionaries and many Congolese were killed; much property was destroyed. We learned that even a concrete building will burn if soaked in gasoline. Missionaries from across the river began to flee, and we discussed whether we should evacuate.

Now I'm quite sure it was before this happened that a little revival had begun among the missionaries. One missionary couple, Norm and Von, made a room behind their house available as a prayer chamber, and we had a kind of prayer vigil there, with different people scheduled for different times.

It was after missionary prayer meeting at Norm and Von's that we had this conversation about whether to evacuate. I didn't want to. After the meeting it happened to be my turn to use the prayer room. While I was praying I began to hear a lot of noise down by the river. No, I wasn't afraid. I wasn't? My heart started beating faster, and that perspiration couldn't be blamed entirely on the muggy atmosphere. And what turned out to be the cause of the commotion? The riverboat had docked, and the usual crowd had gathered.

In February it was decided that women and children should leave the station. The high school principal (Congolese) said to me, "We'd like to be able to leave too."

"Yes, of course you would. I hope you won't need to." All the missionaries could be flown out and even repatriated if necessary. If MAF started flying Congolese to the city, where would they stop?

We arrived in Leopoldville to find many other evacuees from other missions there. Americans who lived in the city had contributed clothes so that those who had fled with nothing would have something to wear. We were not in that situation; nothing of ours had been destroyed, and we'd each been able to bring out a small suitcase. There were a lot of us. It may have been Margaret who asked me, "Would you be willing to go to Sona Bata with Marjorie and Jimmy? Grace can stay at the hostel. Bob's already there."

"Yes, that would be good. I know the station and the language. I'll feel more comfortable there than crowding a family in Leopoldville." I didn't realize for many years how hard it was for Grace to be unceremoniously assigned to the hostel with her parents in two other places. She was especially afraid for her dad left at Vanga.

At Sona Bata the Coop was empty. It was a big rambling house where two single missionaries ordinarily lived. For some reason, not even one was there at that time. Missionaries provided the furniture the children

113

and I needed, and there we were. And thoughtful Jeannette gave me something to do—teach psychology to the nursing students. I had taken one psychology course in college. She gave me a book. I'm not sure what the girls learned. I was also provided with a man to cook and clean and wash. He also watched the children while I taught my one class.

Jimmy was eight months old. He wasn't nursing very much, so I weaned him at Sona Bata. I used to say I weaned him to the thumb because he drank so little from a cup at that time. But he survived and grew to be 6' 2½" and valedictorian of his high school class, so I guess he didn't suffer from malnutrition. Another thing he did at Sona Bata was crawl to the back door, push open the screen door and fall off the steps. That didn't slow him down either.

Even with my psychology class I found life pretty limited with no one over three to talk with at home. God provided for that need too. Two other missionary wives came to Sona Bata to have babies and stayed with me at the Coop while they recovered. First came Gloria with her baby; she left and Trissie brought new little John. So there were three babies at the Coop during that evacuation period. The men left at Vanga decided they should pare their number down so those left could fit in one MAF plane if they needed to evacuate. They had to eliminate only one man, and Norm was chosen. After all, he was the second doctor, and of course he was also crippled with polio. So he left Vanga by plane and enjoyed visiting Boko and other places as the plane picked up other evacuees. Then he finally arrived at Sona Bata, and I was no longer lonely.

After two months away from our stations we all went to missionary retreat in the city. People planning the gathering had decided to have three speakers on successive days and name a reactor to react to each speech. Norm was chosen to speak one day, with Janie as his reactor. Janie had great gifts and great energy. Later, working with student wives at the seminary in the city, she produced the most powerful Easter play I've ever seen. She asked her cast, "Have you ever seen a play in Congo that wasn't a success?" No. "Have you ever seen one that accomplished its aim?" Another story. It's so much fun to make people laugh, and so easy to make them laugh, for instance, at the soldiers trembling and falling down when the angel comes to open the tomb. Janie got the people to keep their minds on what they wanted the play to accomplish. It was shown in the city and televised, and we saw it on TV the following Easter in Kimpese. Janie also prepared Sunday School lessons for Congo, lessons on the same theme for all the different ages. This filled a great need.

Back in 1964, Norm introduced his talk by saying, "Each of us speakers has a reactor, but I'm the only one with an atomic reactor." That brought the desired reaction. But it was April Fool's Day, and Norm thought of a good April Fool. We were all expecting to return to our stations after the retreat, so everyone was surprised when Norm announced seriously, "We've received word from Valley Forge (our mission headquarters) that we are all to return to the States immediately, turning over our work to the Canadian Baptists."

Surprise. Consternation. Wonder. Why would the Canadians be able to stay if we had to leave?

In the back of the church where we were meeting, I had just heard news that made me think, "Oh, dear, he shouldn't be making an April Fool joke at a time like this." Congolese were passing around the word that Pastor Lubikulu had just died. His name means "forgiveness." He's the only Congolese I've ever heard of with that name. He was an old, highly respected, beloved pastor. Jeannette was crying. Then we found out that Tata Lubikulu's death was also an April Fool. Perhaps he had been dying every April Fool's day for a while. Pastor Lubikulu lived a while longer, and we did go back to our homes and our work.

God brought at least one good thing out of the rebellion. In some cases Catholic and Protestant missionaries found themselves refugees together for the duration. Up until that time each group had distrusted the other, feeling pretty sure that those who didn't believe like them were lost. Now Protestants and Catholics found out to their surprise and joy that the others were Christians too.

CHAPTER ELEVEN

One-Hand Surgery

After two years at Vanga we went back to Moanza. The nurse who performed surgery there, Kitswaka, had gone to the States for training, as Kimpiatu had done before. Now Norm was to resume responsibility for the hospital there, doing surgery with his one good hand and the aid of a capable nurse named Mukengele.

The Moanza people who had said, "We're sure you'll be coming back" were very surprised when we actually did return. People had spread the rumor: "That young fellow who was cooking for them paid to have some witchcraft done. The penalty for not following all the rules was this curse on his employer." Come back to the same place where you'd been cursed? Never! Norm surprised them.

The year before, Leon had begun a junior high school at Moanza. Now it became my responsibility to head it up, one section each of seventh and eighth grades.

But between Vanga and Moanza we took a month's vacation at the coast. In those days it was cheap to stay at the hotel at Moanda. That month is memorable for two things. First, most of the family got sick.

The night we slept in Leopoldville on our way down toward the coast Norm complained, "My chest feels as if an elephant was sitting on it." He had an X-ray done at the general hospital. Nothing specific was found, and by the next day he felt better, so we resumed our journey. For the following year he felt unwell off and on; we didn't find out why until we went back to the States on home assignment and he had a stool examination! Working in water for the construction of the Leaning Tower in the valley at Vanga, he had picked up a parasite called *strongyloides* (threadworm). That night in the capital city the larvae were migrating through his lungs. Later on the symptoms were different. Once it was diagnosed, he took the proper treatment and was cured. The *strongyloides* did put an end to his asthma for a number of years!

Down at the coast, it was the turn of the two younger children, Marjorie and Jimmy. They both contracted measles, one after the other. Measles in Congo seems to be more severe than it is in the States. Usually this is thought to be because most Congolese children are not as well-nourished as American kids, but now our own children were having it hard. However, they both got over it, and because we were at the coast for a whole month, there was time for everyone to have some fun. I don't remember my getting sick, or Bob either. Grace waited till the day we left and had an upset stomach on the way.

The other memorable event was much more pleasant. Norm took the two older kids deep-sea fishing, with a guide, of course. Neither of the males caught anything, but slim, 12-year-old Grace snagged a 4-pound barracuda and a 37-pound ocean perch. The guide grabbed her pole and pulled them in for her. The hotel kitchen staff prepared the barracuda for our family's lunch and in the evening brought in a huge platter of perch, which served many of the diners. (We still had to pay for each meal.)

Grace's surprising catch

Back to work at Moanza. Our tiny junior high consisted of a number of boys in the two classes and five or six girls in the first year. The boys lived in dormitories; the girls were placed in homes, with the idea that they would be more protected that way. One was the pastor's daughter and lived at home; the others had relatives on the station. One of them became pregnant that year anyway.

In those days the US was giving away surplus food to needy countries. Church World Service paid for the ocean transport; all we had to do was get it from the port to our centers. That way we were able to provide those growing boys with nourishing bulgur wheat every day. Unfortunately, they didn't appreciate bulgur wheat. One day as I passed by their open dining area they complained, "This food is terrible; taste it!"

"Does anybody have a clean spoon?" No one did, so I went home and got one. When I returned five minutes later I was unable to taste the unpalatable food because it had all been eaten.

We were three teachers—Joy and I and a new high school graduate named Reuben. The rule was that any student who completed secondary studies in our union school at Kimpese owed a year of teaching to the church community before he went on to university or another job. Many young men fulfilled this obligation grudgingly; Reuben was different. He willingly took on whatever we gave him, and did more. He taught science and of course the boys' PE, maybe second year math. He was gifted in music, but music was not required and drawing was, so I assigned him drawing. That was not an intelligent decision. He did his best. Fortunately he organized a choir outside of class and got wonderful music out of the students. Joy taught French and religion. I should have insisted she take drawing too; she would have taught it well. I had history, first year math, and girls' PE. Anyone who knew me would have laughed his or her head off at the idea of my teaching PE. The girls did enjoy having a tailor make shorts for them. I was doing exercises for my back and had the girls do them too. Later we branched out into something a little more exciting. I thought I was a fairly good runner; in the States I had paced Bob as he prepared for a race. The slowest girl was miles ahead of me. The fastest girl looked like an Olympic runner to me, but her brother in second year left her far behind.

How they grew in junior high school! We followed the European system: students rose to speak in class. One day a seventh-grade boy in the last seat was saying something, and I told him, "Stand up, Ndombe."

"Madame, I am standing up," he replied.

The eighth graders looked like giants in comparison. They loved soccer and looked forward to playing against other schools. I learned to hope—maybe pray—that the match would end in a tie. Otherwise the supporters of the losing team were likely to surge onto the field and start a fight. There was also the danger that the home team would bury a fetish under the goal posts. The boys felt sure the priest blessed the ball before they played a Catholic school. Once they asked me to catch the ball and return it to them before they left for a Catholic station. If I could do it again I would pray over it, "Father God, bless both teams, help them to do their best and love each other and make our guys magnanimous in victory (How would I say 'magnanimous' in Kikongo?) or mature and friendly in defeat."

One part of the seventh-grade math curriculum was the concept of negative numbers. I related it to the years BC in history. One day the pastor in charge of Marriage and Family Life for the whole field visited Moanza. He was a wonderful Christian man; you could just feel the love pour out of him as he came in and ascended the platform. Men and women sat separately in church; he encouraged them to sit together and to sing (in their language), "The more we get together the happier we'll be. For your children are my children, and my children are your children; your money is my money, and my money is your money, and the more we get together, the happier we'll be." Good concepts for a Congolese couple. But at one point he wanted to say that something had happened BC. He explained it this way: "Before Christ, people told time backwards. If this year (1965) were BC, it would be 5691." I observed my students murmuring to each other. They may not have

Investing in the next generation

121

understood negative numbers and time Before Christ very well, but they were quite sure that the pastor did not have it right.

In eighth-grade history we took a look at various civilizations and were encouraged to make value judgments about them. On the final exam I mentioned several of these civilizations of various periods and asked the students to say one thing that was good and one thing that was bad about each of them. Just for fun I included the contemporary US. Their response: "Good: They share their things with others." (They knew where the food in their refectory came from.) "Bad: They think they're the greatest!"

I thought about that response quite a bit. Years later, back at Sona Bata, I told it to a group of Swedes and Germans gathered around our table, and asked, "Don't the people of every country think theirs is the greatest?"

One of the Germans replied, "We don't—not since World War II." Were they ashamed of what Hitler had done or of being defeated in the war?

At Moanza that year Marjorie started school. How proudly she went off to kindergarten with her little bottle of water and a rag! The school at that time provided each child with a slate and a slate pencil; all they had to furnish was the wherewithal to clean the slate. About 10:00 a.m. the first day the teacher let the children out for recess; Marjorie thought school was over and came home. She cheerfully went back when she realized her error. That day she came home reciting, *"Deux plus deux égale gatre"* (2 + 2 = 4, with a slight error in pronunciation). The last day of kindergarten she came home reciting, *"Deux plus deux égale gatre."* Obviously her academic progress in that school year was not spectacular, but I'm glad she had the experience.

Back to Reuben. In high school at Kimpese, between Leopoldville and the coast, where education and Christian training had had time to exercise more influence, he had adopted the scientific method. He no longer believed in the power of witchcraft. But on his way home, he had got no farther than Leopoldville before family and friends from Moanza counseled him, "You'd better get yourself a fetish for protection before you go back to Moanza."

Reuben reported to us later, "I saw that no one had just one fetish, so I realized they didn't trust fully in any of them." Reuben came back without a fetish.

Then one day he got sick. In fact, he went off his rocker. He had malaria; that can make one susceptible to all sorts of things. When he went to the outhouse, he felt there was an evil spirit waiting for him inside. We heard about this on Sunday and prayed for Reuben in our missionary prayer meeting that evening, and he got better. But after a few days he relapsed. By this time Norm was away on a trip. I called together several people, missionaries and Congolese, who I thought were powerful in prayer, and we prayed intensively for Reuben. This time he got well and stayed well. The next week we had to meet again, with Reuben, to thank God for healing him. And thus was born the most exciting prayer group I can remember. We had come together because of a need, and none of us ever wanted to miss a meeting. Our group gradually grew until we numbered about a dozen. We took a long time praying because someone would introduce a subject of prayer and everyone would pray about that before we went to another topic.

After several months one of the members reported a problem. Someone—maybe several people—had heard about our group and were jealous because they had not been included. The member immediately invited them, "Come join us!"

But they said, "No, you didn't include us in the beginning." This member suggested that instead of continuing our original group, each one of us form a new prayer group. Moanza had tried cottage prayer meetings before. We agreed to do that.

Well, some groups succeeded and some didn't. Reuben's did; mine didn't. Our group was supposed to meet in a different home each week. One evening as I approached the house where we were to gather, I heard someone say, "Oh, here comes Mama Abell. We have to pray."

After that I wrote a note to each member of our group, saying, "I see that this way of praying does not appeal to you, and I don't want to force you. However, if any of you want to pray with me, you're welcome to come to my house, or I'll come anywhere you say."

One man responded in high dudgeon that I had intimated he didn't want to pray. But while I was still reading his note, all the women in the group appeared at my door! So our women's prayer group started, and grew. We would meet once a week in one of our homes, and we would also go to the hospital and pray for patients there. In one of our weekly meetings one of the women prayed honestly, "Thank you, God, for healing Mama Mpasi. We didn't think you would, but you did it anyway."

One day Norm came home from the hospital in the middle of the morning to ask me to pray with him. A woman had come from a village quite far away, bearing on her back her sixteen-year-old daughter, Nkeni, who looked about ten. Something was wrong with her leg; the mother hoped the doctor would put some salve on it. What was wrong was a sarcoma, which had almost certainly metastasized. Norm wanted guidance as to whether he should amputate the leg, since it seemed virtually certain that the cancer would kill the girl anyway. We prayed together, and Norm went back and took off the leg.

The next day or so a group of pastors, including my dad, who was visiting us, went to the hospital and prayed for Nkeni with laying on of hands. We women came later to pray. I didn't understand the girl's language, but she told one of us, "Something happened to me when the pastors prayed." She recovered quickly and well from the operation and went home with her mother.

Many months later Norm was traveling when a man flagged down his pickup to say, "I want to pay my bill." It was Nkeni's father.

"Could I see your daughter?" Norm asked eagerly.

"Oh, I'll send for her. She's in the field with her mother." Before long she came swinging along on her crutches, smiling and in good health. Norm took a picture. It's too bad he hadn't taken a "before" photo, because people in the States who saw the "after" one were impressed by how thin she was. But that's the normal thinness of people who work hard and eat one meal a day, based on what the women grow in their gardens. Once in a while a man brings home a little game from the forest or fish from the river. Nkeni was well. We were not able to claim a five-year cure because the next year she died in a flu epidemic. But something had happened when people prayed, in her body and in her spirit.

That year my parents came by ship to visit us. They arrived in October. Mother cooked our Thanksgiving turkey. (The station mason also raised sheep and turkeys.) At one point Mother told us, "I think the oven has got a little too hot." Our stove was wood-burning.

So I asked the cook, "Tata, open the oven door a bit for a little while." When we got home from church the door was still open! But the turkey eventually got done, and we had a fine feast.

In our junior high curriculum English was optional. We two missionaries didn't feel we had time to add it to our other responsibilities, but while Mother was there the students had English every day. Mother and Dad had studied French in night school before coming, and Mother had learned quite a bit, at age 70, but of course her spoken French was limited. Our students were very surprised when she wrote something on the blackboard in beautifully correct French.

Our family of six and Jean's parents, in their 70's

Unfortunately Dad had picked up hepatitis on the ship, and at Moanza it made itself known. He wasn't very sick, but when he expressed a craving for steak I got suspicious. I had learned that people with hepatitis feel a need for meat. Norm was away; I radioed him my concern, and he told me to try the ketchup bottle test. I put Dad's urine in one ketchup bottle and mine in another, capped them and shook them both up. Sure enough, the foam on mine was white, but Dad's was yellow. It's wonderful how you can make diagnoses without a lab.

Mother and Dad were staying in another house, although eating with us, and of course Mother took care of Dad. By Christmas time Dad was well, and he and Mother flew to Kikongo to visit that station. (Kikongo is the name of the language the Bakongo speak and also the name of a mission station.) There Mother arrived with both malaria and hepatitis. She was much sicker than Dad. They stayed in the Congo five months instead of three, but when they got back to the States their doctor pronounced them in better health than he had seen them before they left.

⸎

By the way, Reuben told us later that about the same time we had been praying for him, his family had given a goat to the uncle who claimed to have caused his illness. How would one prove which was responsible for his healing?

Once at school something was missing and we couldn't find out which boy had taken it. Reuben suggested, "Let's have each boy touch a doll, telling them the doll will tell us who was the thief."

I protested, "We don't believe in witchcraft."

Reuben countered, "But the boys do." Foolishly I accepted the ploy. It didn't work. We never did find the culprit.

April Fool's Day came. Congolese loved *poisson d'avril* ("April fish" it's called in French). Norm was away. Besides having charge of the hospital, he visited outlying dispensaries, as at Sona Bata. And occasionally he went to the city or to another church center for some reason. One of our schoolboys knocked on my door at 6:00 a.m., before I had my thinking cap on. He brought the following note (I translate): "Madame Abell, I have the honor to report to you that Mr. Solo has hit Pika. What are you going to do about it?" This was really incredible, because gentle little Mr. Solo, the man in charge of the boys' dorms, would never hit anyone—but if any of the boys could stimulate such a reaction it would be Pika.

While I was still absorbing that news, someone else came to tell me my office at school was in complete disarray; someone had got into it during the night. So I took my little self up to the school. I had never been there that early in the morning and was surprised to see a steady stream of boys going from their dorm area to the dispensary. It turned out to be sick call. I had no idea so many of them asked for medicine on a given day. The other people about were women sweeping the ground in front of the church building. As I drew nearer I heard the boys shouting joyously, *"Bien avalé!"* but I didn't understand it until

I looked at my office. It was indeed a mess, but it was the same mess I'd left it in the night before. *Bien avalé* means "well swallowed." This April fish had swallowed the bait—hook, line, and sinker.

At some time Reuben confided in me, "I can't talk to a girl without people thinking there's something between us. I'm used to the way they do things at Kimpese, where boys and girls talk freely together. I think that's a lot healthier. It helps make the sexes more equal, too." But it wasn't accepted at Moanza. So before the year was out, for self-protection, he said, he and Malia announced their engagement. She was the prettiest of the girl students and the daughter of a chief who lived in the village up on the hill. Her mother was a very nice woman, having to deal with another wife in the same compound.

The end of the school year came. Now in Congo the teachers gave final exams, then the pupils came back to school for a few more days while the teachers figured out their grades. It's a complicated process because some classes are taught more than five times a week and some less, so the grades are weighted accordingly. You don't just base everything on 100 and then average them out. But I thought it was silly to make kids come back after exams with no motivation and make teachers teach while struggling with their grades. I thought we three teachers could get our grades together in one evening. Well, Joy and I did all right, but poor Reuben got so sleepy he made several mistakes. By the time I discovered them the kids had already received their grades and it was too late to do anything about it.

Wherever we lived in Congo, we had people helping us in the house. We didn't call them servants; of course they were. We called them helpers or workers. They were that too. In the early days of mission work it was considered an honor and a boon to work in a missionary's house. A promising student could earn his school fees and learn a lot from working in a missionary home. Such a job was no longer prestigious in our day, but it certainly was useful. I'm a slow worker at best. If I had had to make all our meals, using a wood stove, and do the laundry by hand, ironing with a charcoal iron, I would have had no time left to teach or do anything else. So I appreciated our cook and wash jack. At Vanga and Moanza we also had a baby sitter for Jimmy when I was at school. It would have been good if we had always spoken Kikongo, or whatever the local language was, with each other when any of our help was within earshot. It would have been respectful, and they wouldn't have thought they needed to learn English to find out the secrets we were hiding from them. People at Moanza were sure they knew about our secret worship. During our first term the missionaries enjoyed an occasional hot dog roast on a small level area a little bit down toward the river from our house, in the opposite direction from the rest of the station. We would take the trouble to keep the grass mown and, before the picnic, use insect spray, then make the fire and toast our (canned) frankfurters and eat the picnic there outdoors, with a wonderful view of the ranges of hills across the river. Well, why in the world would people who had kitchens and dining rooms eat outdoors when they didn't have to? And they eat those things that look like people's fingers and probably are. This must be where they get their secret power by which they get so rich.

Well, let's get back to house helpers. Unfortunately it was all too easy to speak our native language among ourselves, so we missed that opportunity for a Christian witness.

Our cook at Moanza that year was a young man named Sammy. He was always cheerful and a good worker. When I dashed off to school before he came to work, without leaving him instructions for the day, he would present himself at my classroom door to ask what he should prepare. We got along very well.

Sammy's brother had been a village catechist. Such a man is responsible for the church and primary school (two grades) in a village that does not have a pastor. He works hard and is paid very little. It's a labor of love for the people and for the Lord. This catechist married Suzanne and they had three children. Then he died of tuberculosis, which is common where people are malnourished. Kongo tradition is like that of the Old Testament Hebrews: when a man dies, his brother is to take the widow as his wife. Where people have accepted monogamy, this is seldom possible as the brothers are usually already married, but in this case Sammy was single and took sweet Suzanne as his wife. Suzanne had already come to Moanza and been hired as a hospital worker. She had no training; she learned on the job. Her wedding gown was made of White Cross gauze. When our senior missionary heard that, she wished she had known so she could have provided Suzanne with something nicer.

Now Sammy was also a village catechist, but Suzanne was making more money than he, so it made sense for him to apply for a job at Moanza. That's how he ended up cooking for us.

Of course they had the three children sired by Sammy's brother, but naturally Sammy wanted children of his own. They didn't come right away. When little Noel was born at Christmas time, we all rejoiced with that family. Sadly, at about six months he fell ill with what turned out to be meningitis. Meningitis is hard to diagnose, and when it was identified it wasn't possible to save little Noel. The whole station mourned with them.

One day some women came to tell me, "We need to carry water for Mama Suzanne." Traditionally a woman who lost a child was to mourn that child for a whole year, staying in her house. That meant she couldn't work her gardens or go to the stream to do dishes or get water. Her "sisters" did that for her. By the time I found out about this custom, the year had been sensibly reduced to about a month. I willingly carried my pail of water on my head (having to hang on, as no one else did), but by the time we got to Mama Suzanne's house it was no more than half full. A good thing she didn't have to depend on missionary sisters!

Some time later, the women came back and told me, "It's time to bring Mama Suzanne out of mourning."

She welcomed us into her home but insisted, "I'm not ready to come out of mourning yet." She sat on the floor with her legs straight out in front of her and said, "I've been reading the Book of Job." Then she shared what she'd been learning. About a week later she was ready to come out of mourning.

After we had left Moanza, we came back for a visit and went to Sammy and Suzanne's house to talk and pray with them. We were all kneeling on the floor, holding hands and praying, when a cockroach crawled under my skirt. I did not scream, but my prayer was seriously interrupted. My legendary Aunt Fanny Tenney, in New York State some generations earlier, would have been grievously disappointed in me. When a mouse crawled up under her long, heavy skirt in church, she may have stopped worshiping, but no one else would have known it as she grasped that mouse in her hand through the skirt and squeezed until it died, presumably without a single squeak.

CHAPTER TWELVE

Tour of the Congo

If you put your thumb down on the middle of a map of Africa, it will also be in the middle of the Democratic Republic of the Congo, a country as large as the US east of the Mississippi, inhabited by tribes speaking more than 200 different languages. The Congo is shaped like a question mark on its side, the stem pointing west as the Congo River makes its abundant way to the Atlantic Ocean. The river begins as the Lualaba in the mountains of the southeast corner of the country. Flowing north and then west, the mighty river approaches the northern border of the country. The equator crosses it here; this is the dense equatorial rain forest. As the river makes its way south, dry season appears. Here the rainy season is interrupted and the vegetation becomes grassy savannah with forests in the river valleys.

In 1878 the first missionaries entered the Congo. Over the years one denomination after another, one country after another, sent its own missionaries, and gradually more and more parts of the country began to light up with the Good News. The Belgian Congo required the Protestant missions to form one umbrella organization to deal with the government. Thus the Congo Protestant Council (CPC) was born. The various missions divided up responsibility for the many areas of the country so that missions were not competing with each other. Most missions started churches, schools, and some sort of medical work.

In 1966 a missionary doctor named David was trying to cover the Medical Office of the CPC in addition to his other responsibilities. Hearing that it was no longer appropriate for Dr. Abell to be in charge of a hospital, including surgery, he suggested to the Congolese Director of CPC, "Why don't we try to get Dr. Abell as the first full-time Director of the Medical Office?"

"That's a good idea," Dr. Shaumba agreed. "I'll get in touch with Chet and see if his board will second him to us."

It was arranged, and Norm was adjusting to the prospect of an administrative job in the capital in 1967. Before that, on furlough, he planned to take a public health course at Harvard. In the meantime an exciting development was added to the mix.

The National Council of Churches in New York City was planning a month-long survey of medical institutions in the Congo. Dr. Nute

Dr. Abell, Dr. Nute, and the MAF pilot

was chosen to conduct the survey, but he needed someone familiar with medical work in the country to guide him. Who more appropriate than Dr. Abell?

The children and I returned to the States in August, while Norm and Dr. Nute prepared for their tour of the Congo in September. They visited some 30 institutions—Protestant, Catholic, and government—hospitals and training centers ranging from two-year nurses' courses to the medical school in the southeast corner of the country. Dr. Nute wrote up his notes on the plane between destinations. Norm waited until the tour was over, then had a big job writing up his report and getting it submitted.

After the tour came a meeting with 23 missionary doctors in Leopoldville, then contact with the General Secretary of the National Health Ministry. Mr. Ngandu was eager to cooperate with the Protestant Medical Office, which would be Norm's responsibility. So September and October rolled by. But Norm still had tasks to accomplish at Moanza, turning the medical responsibility over to nurse Kitswaka, setting up the new autoclave, straightening accounts, installing a new generator, working on wiring. This was complicated by transportation difficulties. The truck didn't arrive; the driver was sick. The MAF plane that was to take Norm to Moanza was needed for a family. George, who would have worked with Norm on the generator and wiring, left the same day Norm arrived. That meant that Norm had to do all the work by himself. He didn't leave things undone, he just stayed until they were done. As it turned out, he started his furlough in mid-November.

CHAPTER THIRTEEN

Meanwhile, Back in the States

Having stayed in Judson House in Malden during our first furlough, this time we were in Newell House in Newton Center, another residence our board kept for missionaries on furlough. Malden is a northern suburb of Boston. Newton Center lies southwest of the city. Its school system is such that Harvard professors like to live there so their children can start preparing for Harvard in first grade. Fortunately, neither our children nor I understood this right away. Later on I attended a parent-teacher meeting in which one father asked if he should learn "new math" while his child was being exposed to it. The thoughtful reply came back, "Only if you would learn Russian while your child was studying it."

Our new abode was a two-story, yellow clapboard house with two-car garage. We lived on the first floor this time. Upstairs was a family fresh from a term in Japan, deeply committed Christians, delightful neighbors. Andover-Newton Theological School is located in Newton Center. This couple knew a young Japanese woman studying there. She found her studies difficult, and they kept a very close watch on her, since in Japanese culture suicide is an approved method of reacting to failure. Once when we'd been talking about higher criticism (of the Bible) and the doubts it aroused in some pastoral students, our neighbor said about her husband, "They could prove the whole Bible was false from cover to cover, and it wouldn't affect his faith one bit. He knows his God."

The couple had five children, two older boys and three younger girls. Betsy, the oldest girl, had a crisis early in our stay. The doctor who gave her the school exam in Newton Center took her off the medication she'd been taking, and one day she was in trouble. Her dad was not at home, and her mother asked me if I would drive them to Children's Hospital in Boston. I agreed, of course, but was very relieved when another friend offered to make the trip instead.

The second daughter, Mary, was Marjorie's age, and they became good friends. Suzie, the youngest, was four, and our Jimmy had turned three in July. Suzie thought the sun rose and set in Jimmy Abell. In Sunday School, if her class was going outdoors she wouldn't go unless Jimmy's class was going too.

Bob started his sophomore year in high school. Junior high went through ninth grade, so all the sophomores were new to that impressively large school. One of his classmates asked Bob, "Where are you from?" meaning one of the two junior highs that fed the high school.

"Congo."

"Huh?"

"Congo, Africa."

"You mean with all those wild animals?" But it turned out the Newton Center kids weren't really interested in Africa. Another MK (missionary kid), Ted, lived in the area and would sometimes attend the church youth group with Bob. They occasionally talked to each other in Kituba or Lingala. That did not endear them to the girls they were cultivating friendships with.

Bob asserted one day, "That is not a youth group." What he meant was that it wasn't like the one he had known in Kinshasa. Kinshasa? Yes. Now, in 1966, the President changed the names of the largest cities from European to African; Leopoldville became Kinshasa. That made sense. Why should the independent Congo still call its capital city by the name of the Belgian king who exploited it as his personal possession until 1908?

Massachusetts was a lot more worldly than the Kinshasa our children knew. But the Baptist youth group in Newton Center did some good things. Once the youth group was in charge of the morning service. Bob was chosen to give the message, on Jonah. He left the congregation with the challenge: "Where is your Nineveh?" The only problem was that he almost passed out. It has something to do with being long and lanky, standing still for quite a while—and probably, adolescence and nervousness.

Getting back to the beginning of school, the guidance counselor expressed admiration for Bob's grades from The American School of Kinshasa (TASOK). Bob replied, "You should see my sister."

The counselor was so supportive. She told him, "We find that boys often bloom later than girls." And sure enough, Grace was the valedictorian of her high school class, but it was Bob who graduated from college summa cum laude.

At open house we parents were invited to follow an abridged version of our child's daily schedule, visiting each classroom and meeting each teacher. Thanks to Bob, we escaped getting lost. The biology teacher told us, "Teaching biology has changed a lot since you went to school.

You probably studied each of the phyla. Now we talk about what the DNA and the RNA are doing."

I wanted to ask, "What are they doing?"

One time Bob told that teacher, "I'm pleased that you don't talk about the conflict between faith and science."

The teacher responded, "I don't think there is any." Good for you!

Grace was in eighth grade. The school had wonderful opportunities. There were elective mini-courses one could take. One was on math games, another on Shakespeare. Grace studied "Richard III." In home economics, we studied sewing in my day; Grace's course was called Clothing. She made a pleated skirt. She had carefully marked the material following the pattern, when the teacher told her, "Since it's plaid material, you follow the lines of the plaid"; Grace did it all over. Of course, if you follow the lines of the plaid, the skirt doesn't get any wider as it goes down and you can't put it on. She did it a third time. At the end of the course the teacher evaluated each student and also asked them to evaluate the course, telling what they had learned. Grace wrote that she had learned patience.

One day the English teacher asked the students to write their impression of the objective case. Grace told what the objective case was, how it was used. No, the teacher wanted her impression of the objective case. Grace didn't have a clue, and I couldn't think how to elicit an impression from her, so I suggested, in a tearful voice, "I'm the objective case. I never get to do anything. People just do things to me." I suppose I wasn't the only parent to supply a child with an answer.

Marjorie started first grade, but that year got interrupted. After six years since her birth and an early consultation with a pediatrician, the general practitioner we went to for our furlough physicals diagnosed a congenital condition that required surgery. She spent two weeks in the hospital. She was in a ward with several other children. The charge nurse came in and told the children, "My name is Kitty, and when you want me you just call, 'Here, kitty, kitty!'" There was a playroom full of lovely toys. Marjorie loved the hospital; she didn't want to come home!

In PE Bob was playing a game in which two basketballs were in the air at once. Bob had caught one when another came at him. Trying to handle that, he broke his thumb. The school called me. I think we did not yet have a car; it seems to me I had to get a taxi to go to the school and take Bob to an orthopedist. He X-rayed the thumb, set it, and X-rayed it again. The thumb was nicely put back in its proper position. Unfortunately, there is no way to keep a thumb in its proper position, so Bob still has a slightly misshapen thumb.

Norm hoped we could all meet him on his arrival in New York City Armistice Day, 1966, but it didn't work out. For one thing, I don't think we got a car until he came. Now he was permitted to drive if he had automatic shift or a steering knob. Our car that year was a pale blue, used Volkswagen Bug. Since it was a bug and pretty colorless, we named it *Mbembele*, which means "mosquito." Bob taught himself to drive by turning Mbembele around in the garage. At Christmas time we visited Norm's brother and family in Philadelphia. The kids enjoyed getting acquainted with their Philadelphia cousins. In addition to the six of us, we took suitcases, of course, our contribution of food, Christmas presents, and Bob's guitar. We must have had a roof rack, and Marjorie and Jimmy traveled in the well behind the back seat. When it came time to set out, I couldn't find the grapes I was to take.

After we returned, they came to light in a low cupboard. I think Jimmy had changed their abode. Sadly, they had to be thrown out.

That was really an eventful year for Bob. He found he could rent a guitar to buy, so he did, and taught himself to play it. That guitar stayed with him through college until he needed to buy an engagement ring for his intended. Then the guitar was sacrificed for the greater need—but Anna's wedding present to him was a new guitar.

A less happy event for Bob was orthodontia. It was high time he had it. We contacted an orthodontist as soon as possible, but it was nip and tuck as to whether he could complete the work before we needed to leave. He offered a reduction in the price if Bob would be willing to have the work done faster (and more painfully). It was rough, but Bob and the orthodontist did it.

Of course it was too late for Norm to work on his Master of Public Health in the fall semester. He took the opportunity to have some corrective surgery done. Since polio his left arm had been pretty useless. Now a surgeon proposed to transplant a tendon so that he would be able to carry something, such as a briefcase, with that arm. That seemed pretty useful, so Norm underwent the operation, which involved opening the arm to the elbow. He recovered from that in time to enter the second semester at Harvard, but it really didn't help much without the first semester.

And what did I do? Well, take care of my husband and four children. One day Jimmy and Susie were playing in our bedroom. I heard Susie exclaim happily, "Your mommy's going to like this snowstorm!" They had opened at least one of the pillows and were enjoying letting the feathers fly around the room. It was winter; they were wearing fuzzy clothes.

No, Susie, Jimmy's mommy does not particularly enjoy this snowstorm.

∞

As usual, Marjorie's birthday came so early in the school year she hadn't had time to make friends yet. For Bob's December birthday we invited his MK (missionary kid) friends and also a classmate Bob had been befriending. Grace warned us that that boy would spoil the party, and in a way he did. He asked who had catered the meal. I suppose that was a compliment. We all went to see *The Sound of Music,* which he pronounced "pure schmaltz."

∞

One Sunday I attended the old ladies' class in the First Baptist Church. The teacher encouraged us to expect God to do something special in our lives the next day. Well, the next day a woman telephoned me and asked if she could come over, would I be her friend. I had spoken in the church where she was Director of Christian Education. She did come, and we did become friends. I wasn't good about sensing people's needs and reaching out to them, so God put her in my lap. She had had a very traumatic life. Her husband was dead; she had one daughter who suffered from a congenital condition that made her bones break very easily. When Grace's birthday came along, she invited that girl and two classmates, one of whom was Jewish. First we drove to a nearby town to attend an outdoor event. It was a cold, rainy day, not very pleasant. Then we went home and made pizza. Grace's other friend had thought the Jewish one was not kosher, and we were putting sausage in the pizza. She said the smell made her sick, and she went home! Not a successful birthday party.

I didn't do a lot of deputation that furlough, but one time I was to speak at a church in Lynn, on the northeastern edge of the Greater Boston area. Mbembele did not possess a fuel gauge. Instead she had a spare gas tank which was supposed to hold about a gallon. On the trip around the circumferential, Rte. 128, the gas ran out and we (the car and I) switched to the auxiliary tank. Soon a sign for a service area came up and I prepared to turn off. But there was also an exit nearby, and I managed to take the exit instead of the service area road. By the time I got back on the highway the service area was past. Before another one appeared the engine starved to death. I pulled over to the shoulder and was happy to see a gas station on the road we were going over. I climbed down the embankment and trudged up again with a red can of gasoline. But when it was in the tank, the car still refused to start. I had to make my way back down the embankment and ask for help. Finally I was on my way again, and eventually I reached my destination and parked across the street from the church. Hurrying out of the car, I dropped my box of slides, which popped open, disgorging slides in random order on the pavement. I stuffed them back in the box and hurried into the church, where people were no doubt relieved that they would have a missionary speaker after all. They had reached the dessert course, so I re-sorted slides as I ate my pie and was somewhat bemused when the man who was to run the slide projector asked me, "How shall I show them, one after the other?"

One more memory of that year involves a Lay School of Theology given by Andover-Newton, every evening for a week or maybe two. I took a course given by Nels Ferré, and another in Old Testament. The two profs were both delightful and very different. The OT professor started at the top left-hand corner of the blackboard and taught very systematically. I remember asking him after class if the stories in the Book of Daniel actually happened. He answered that that wasn't the point. One time he told the class about opening the notebook of a female student and finding she had written on the first page, "He reminds me of a rabbit."

Nels Ferré, on the other hand, said things like, "Karl Barth believes in the Trinity, but not like three billiard balls (here he whirled to the blackboard and drew three contiguous circles), and not like a heavenly committee meeting in which two say to one, 'You go.'"

Someone in another class had asked Ferré, "And what do you believe? Where are you in all this?"

To which Ferré replied, "Square in the middle of God's truth."

Once after class I told Ferré how Bobby, aged four or five, informed his little sister, "God is everywhere. He's right in this sugar bowl."

Grace retorted, "No, he isn't, because if he was I'd eat him up."

The theologian then recounted how his son at age three had hit his head against the wall and announced, "In one sense God is in this wall, and in another sense he isn't."

CHAPTER FOURTEEN

City Dwellers

The school year came to an end. It was 1967, and back to the Congo we went, but this time to an administrative position in the capital city. We were not city dwellers. True, we lived in cities for the first years of our married life, but I had grown up in small towns and Norm had spent some of his happiest years on a farm. Denison University, where we met, is located in a very small town.

Now we were to live in Kinshasa. At independence time it had numbered some 350,000 people, about the same as our beloved Rochester. In the past seven years it had been growing by leaps and bounds.

We must have given our colleagues a hard time. On our arrival the Mission Secretary told us, "There isn't any place for you in the CBCO compound, but we've found a house in Parc Hembise, where the Belgians live." CBCO stood for the Baptist Churches of Western Congo, the denomination started by American Baptists. Our missionaries in Kinshasa lived in that compound.

Instead of expressing our gratitude, I burst out, "Oh, can't we live in the *cité?* We want to have Congolese neighbors, like we did at Sona Bata."

And our good friend the long-suffering Mission Secretary, who knew these crazy Abells, replied, "We'll see what we can do."

Accordingly, we started our Kinshasa chapter in a large house built by Belgians. I deplored the waste space. The man across the street kept several dogs. Now this was a tense time in the Congo. Mercenaries from other countries who had helped the Congo government defeat the Simbas in 1964 were still around, and the government was not paying them. They now rebelled, and white people in general could be suspected of being mercenaries. We were told that the radio encouraged people to: "Take your machetes and drive them out!" The trouble was compounded by the similarity of the words "missionary" and "mercenary," in French as in English. Long-haired teenage sons were especially suspect. Some missionaries had not been allowed to return at this time, and some had been stopped en route. This was the time we visited Rome on the way to Congo. What would we have done if we'd had to cool our heels in Italy?

Some Belgians had sent their wives home from Congo temporarily. In general nerves were on edge, and when the dogs barked at night I woke up and wondered what was happening. After a while we got used to it and slept through.

I did have a somewhat painful introduction to the house. When we first entered, I went around blessing the doors and windows. Then I tackled the old electric stove. Its dials no longer showed when a burner was on, so I tried to turn them on, hoping I'd be able to mark the dials. When I came back I put my hand on one (flat plate over the coils) and found that it was indeed on. We didn't have a refrigerator working yet, and it was one of those times when the water pressure didn't suffice to pump water out of the faucet. I finally found a spigot low down in the garage and an old chamber pot I could fill with water to soak my burned hand.

We lived in that house until Thanksgiving, when our mission secretary found a half house for us in the *cité*, the part of the city where the Congolese lived. This was an old section, and our particular part, called Camp Babylone, had had rather nice but inexpensive houses built by Belgians for Congolese before independence. This one was owned by a school director at Sona Bata, our first station (not the director we had known). He and his family lived in one half, we in the other. It was a two-story house, with living room, dining room, and kitchen on the first floor, four tiny bedrooms and a bath on the second. On the narrow, concrete-floored back porch we put a washer and ironing board, with a foot locker under the ironing board to hold clothes awaiting ironing. There was a fruitful papaya tree in the back yard, but we never got any papayas from it, because we would wait till they were ripe, and in the meantime neighborhood boys would harvest them. One day there were so many boys in the tree that a branch broke under one of them. It wasn't far to the ground; he didn't break any bones.

Remember my blessing the doors and windows of the first house? I prayed that only good would come in through them. That was so as long as we lived there, but while we were moving, thieves came in. For some reason we had stored wrapped Christmas presents on a shelf; no doubt we'd brought them that way from family in the States. The thieves liked those. When they came back for another load, we surprised the thieves, and they left without our seeing them. Unfortunately we didn't think to warn our neighbors, and after leaving us the thieves visited the MAF family living behind us.

The new home had two glaring deficiencies by our American standards. There were no closets, no shelves, no hooks, not a nail in the wall. We put a few shelves under the staircase and made or had made wall bookcases in the living room. Then we wanted an electric stove, but that street had only 220 volts, not the 380 a stove required. They put a line in for us eventually—amazing, come to think of it—but until the new year we did all our cooking on a one-burner hot plate. In the meantime Bob came home from The American School of Kinshasa (TASOK) one day and announced, "I promised to provide the manioc chips for our international feast."

"You did? How much do you need?"

"I dunno. Lots. We don't want to run out." So the cook, Bob, and I spelled each other all day long frying thin slices of manioc in deep fat.

So many memories from that house! The owner's family next door had a daughter about Grace's age, and we rejoiced that Grace would have a Congolese friend—but alas! The other girl's French was so much better than Grace's that Grace was too shy to talk to her. They played together but in silence.

There were plenty of neighbor kids for Marjorie and Jimmy to play with. Marjorie knew we hoped they would learn Lingala, the African language spoken in the city. Even the children of Kikongo-speaking parents spoke Lingala with their peers, to the extent of not understanding when the grownups spoke Kikongo. One day Marjorie came in all excited. "Jimmy's learning Lingala! He said, *"Ici!"* *Ici* means "here"—in French. Jim now informs me that he did learn some words in Lingala—bad ones!

Jimmy started school. When he came home from his first day in kindergarten, I asked him "Jimmy, what did you like best in kindergarten?"

"Rest hour!" At home he didn't get to lie on a towel on the floor while the teacher read to them. Jimmy loved his kindergarten teacher. She was tall and young and very good with the children. The summer following that year she was visiting Israel—Jericho, to be exact—when a stray bullet from across the river struck and killed her.

In kindergarten each child was to make a picture book about his family. Jimmy did fine on the cover, a picture of his house—well, a house, anyhow. Each succeeding page was to have a picture of a family member. Jim's pages were blank. He explained that he couldn't draw people. He could draw bicycles and guns (!), but not people. That got remedied later. In high school he painted both seascapes and action pictures with people in them.

One day the teacher's report stated, "Jimmy never does anything fast—even going out to play." Another time: "Jimmy is very good at making things out of useless materials." That was a skill encouraged in the schools for Congolese children. *Matériaux de fortune* meant whatever they could pick up—twigs, bottle caps—green grapefruit slices made good wheels for toy cars; they didn't need to learn that in school. In fact, kids made amazingly accurate vehicles out of light wood or wire: not just a car, a Volkswagen; not just an airplane, a Cessna 182. When Jim was in high school, his counselor encouraged him with the idea that if he couldn't have his first choice of profession he could become a fabricator—not a liar but someone who makes what he needs with what he has on hand. If he didn't have the tool he needed for a particular job, Jim, like his dad, would make one.

Camp Babylone was in the section of the city called Kintambo, where the American Baptist work had started. The Kintambo church was within walking distance. I trained Sunday School teachers there on a week night, and we took our children there on Sunday mornings. When that service was over we drove downtown to the English-speaking church. After a while I realized it was too much for the kids. Sunday morning was more hassle than worship. So we excused them from going to Kintambo. They enjoyed the English language Sunday School.

My Sunday School responsibilities eventually enlarged. Our colleague Eva, whom we had first known at Sona Bata, was now living in the city and meeting with Sunday School teachers in various parishes around town. American Baptist work had started with the one church in Kintambo; now there were CBCO (Baptist Churches of Western Congo) churches in an ever-increasing number of communes, as the sections of the city were called. Eva turned over another of these Sunday Schools to me, along with some of the responsibility for vacation Bible schools. What fun! Most of the teachers were high school students. At Bandalungwa, my second parish, one student had founded the Sunday School and the youth group and started a ministry to children at the nearby prison. Children in prison? Yes. Some with their mothers, some arrested for vagrancy. The young people brought song and worship to them, also soap and other necessities. Not surprisingly, that young man married a fine Christian young woman and became a leader in the church. There was one girl who didn't join the Sunday School teachers but did teach in Vacation Bible School. She was a fine, intelligent young person. One time we were discussing how we spent our money and she remarked, *"Il faut être belle"* (you have to be beautiful), meaning it's necessary to spend money on cosmetics and hairdressing. That young woman went into Christian work. She visited us years later. She had a ministry to young girls, encouraging them to wait for marriage. She said, "When I talk to 13- and 14-year-olds and see the sad looks on their faces, I realize it's too late to tell them to remain virgins. I need to talk to 10- and 12-year-olds."

At that time the Bandalungwa church did not have a church building. The church met in the courtyard of a relatively well-to-do family. The husband worked at the American embassy. Our Sunday School teachers' class convened on the porch of that home. One evening Norm was busy elsewhere and I had no one to leave the younger children with, so I took them with me. The host family had a litter of puppies; Marjorie carried one around all evening. When I got ready to go, the woman of the house smiled and said to me in her best English, "I give the dog for the children."

Gulp. Nobody had asked me if I was ready for a dog. "Thank you. Is it male or female?"

"It's female."

Gulp. So Spotty came home with us. Later people wondered why she was called Spotty. Her puppy spots had spread out to a general mottled effect. Poor dog! When she went into heat, every dog in the neighborhood treated her like a woman of the streets. Then when she came home, the next-door dog felt sure she was his wife. No peace anywhere. Eventually her first litter announced their arrival. Unfortunately it was at night. Now we had a driveway beside that house but no garage. Bob had got some chicks from fellow missionary Murray and built a small concrete block henhouse at the end of the driveway. While he was building the house the chicks stayed in their box under his bed. Building took longer than he had planned; the chicks grew fast. Everyone drew a sigh of relief when they could finally emigrate to their own dwelling. And for a while Bob had eggs to sell. Then one night thieves came and stole all his roosters. Hens don't lay well when there are no roosters, we found. But to prevent further theft we took to parking our Volkswagen smack in front of the henhouse door. What we didn't realize was that Spotty had carefully dug a hole in the sandy soil of the henhouse floor as a bassinet for her babies. And just when she needed it, she couldn't get in! Our bedroom window looked out on the driveway, but we had an air conditioner in it—the only time we had air conditioning in Congo—so it took a long time for Spotty's frenzied moans to get through the white sound and wake me up. I went down to see what the trouble was and then had to go upstairs again for the car key so I could move the car. Finally the poor mother was able to get to her birthing room. She had already delivered one pup and covered it with sand as best she could. That one was already cold. I think another one died, but there were at least four little roly-poly canines soon moving around. Before they grew very big, tragedy struck again. One by one they died in great pain. The mother grieved for each one, then ate it. In those days the government sent men around to spray the outsides of houses with DDT to keep down mosquitoes. I suspected that Spotty had ingested enough DDT to kill her pups through her milk. People told me that couldn't happen. If not, I can't imagine what killed Spotty's pups. Another time Spotty scared us. After receiving a rabies shot, she gradually became paralyzed. First she was dragging her hind legs behind her; then she couldn't walk at all. We had to bring food and water to her. But gradually she recovered.

Working with Sunday School teachers was rewarding. Traditionally the teacher told the children, *"Kanga maboko"* (fold your arms) and then did all the talking. The children's only participation came in singing, as loudly as possible. When the next-door class wanted to pray, that didn't work too well. I encouraged the teachers to ask the children questions, get them talking, find activities to relate to the story. In our Stateside Sunday Schools, children at least have paper and crayons, often things to cut out. And teachers' books suggest all kinds of activities. These teachers had to dream up their own. We used drama quite a bit, playing the story. And we used what came to hand. Once for the Easter story we made a little garden in the sand, with twigs for trees. Buildings and walls were made of concrete blocks, some with decorative holes in them. A discarded part of a block made the empty tomb.

There was always a pageant or play at Christmas. How people loved to make fun of the census takers, supplying them with adding machines! I saw one Herod lolling on his throne with one or two wives beside him. What troubled me was seeing Mary dragging her way into Bethlehem, her pregnancy almost to the ground, already in labor. I asked them, "Would you make fun of your mother like that?"

The high school students took up new ideas quite well. One older man in the group had a harder time changing. "But the children don't have anything to say."

"No, Tata, you have to get them used to the idea that they can think."

You never know what consequences your teaching may have. In vacation Bible school the rooms were packed with children, especially the youngest ones. I thought one activity pre-schoolers could do would be leaf rubbing, giving each child one crayon and a piece of paper to put over the leaf, but I found even that was hard for them. In another class a pastoral student was supposed to be teaching, but I found him cutting out the letters he should have made the night before. They were to create a hanging with leaves and flowers and a verse praising God for creation. Here was the teacher in a back seat, leaving the children with nothing to do. It was second grade, so I told the teacher, "Give them directions on the blackboard."

"Oh, they can't read," responded the teacher.

So I went to the blackboard and wrote, in their language, "Go outdoors. Get leaves and flowers." To my delight, the children looked at the words, then looked questioningly at me, and started out. I hope that pastoral student learned two things that day.

Then there was the young teacher who came to me with joy, reporting on how he had put my teaching into practice. "I was teaching about Pentecost, so when we came to the tongues of fire I gave each child a match and had them light them and hold them over their heads!"

I was also teaching English in the Kintambo Baptist high school, located next to the church. One time one of my young Sunday School teachers asked if I could get him into my school. I asked the principal if he would give the boy an entrance exam. Instead he just accepted him on my recommendation. I sure wish he hadn't. Come exam time, we teachers monitored each other's exams, and of course we were supposed to prevent cheating. I had learned to be suspicious of long sleeves rolled up. Later I think I had all the boys unroll their sleeves before entering the room. But this time, as soon as everyone had started the French exam, I strode to the back of the room (rather than begin at the front, where all the kids could see what I was doing), and felt in the rolled-up sleeve of the first student I came to, who happened to be my Sunday School teacher. Sure enough, there was a long slip of paper with a list of authors on it. I marched the boy to the front, took his paper, and sent him on his way. It took him a long time to forgive me. I wonder if he thought some magic power had cued me in.

❦

What was Norm doing all this time? He was administering the Medical Department of the CPC. His trip with Dr. Nute had given him an excellent overall picture of the Protestant medical work throughout the country, problems and needs. Perhaps the most important accomplishment of his tenure was the formation of CEPAM, a pharmacy created to supply medicines to Protestant hospitals around the country. Before that, hospitals received some medicines through Interchurch Medical Assistance. Others they had to look for in the commercial pharmacies in the capital. Often the doctor had to make the long journey there and then go the rounds of various pharmacies for several days to try to find what he was lacking. After CEPAM got going, its pharmacist, Warren, had access to European pharmaceutical firms and was able to furnish a more consistent supply.

Another task that Norm enjoyed was orienting new missionary doctors. During their first days in the capital they would come to his office, ask questions, and get briefed for what lay ahead of them. Norm had the right combination of experience on the local level and the overview of hospitals and nursing schools, Protestant, Catholic, and government, to be very helpful to the newbies. Also, he cared about each of them, as well as the Congolese they would work with and those they would minister to.

One day I decided to invite the neighbors on our block to come to our house to pray. After my experience at Moanza, I shouldn't have been surprised that it was the women who came. I asked them, "What would you like to pray about?"

They answered, "Our homes and our families. It's different for us than it is for you. Your husband listens to you."

I remember hearing about a woman whose husband had left her for a younger woman. That happened distressingly often. There came a time when the first wife needed the father of her children. She went to where he was living and called to him. Now in Congo, at least in that part, a person was sometimes addressed as the mother of a child. I might be called Mama Abell, or *Mama Dokuta* (Mrs. Doctor) or Mama Jeanne, but I also could be called *Mam'a Babi* (the mother of Bobby). This woman stood outside her husband's home and called, "Tat'a Catherine! Tat'a Albert! Tat'a Josephine! Tat'a Marc! Tat'a Joseph!" naming each of their children in an effort to get him to respond. He never did.

Our children went to the American school, but we did have Congolese friends. The house on our right was occupied by the wife of a member of Parliament. People were pleased that this Christian man had risen to a significant position in the government, but with worldly advancement had come worldly lifestyle; he was one of those living with a younger, more sophisticated woman. His first wife said he visited her just often enough to keep her pregnant. One thing I remember about her was that she had a hedge of manioc around her house. There was no room in the city for a garden, but she made sure she had some manioc. Otherwise one had to buy everything at the local market, just a few blocks away.

The house on the other side was occupied by an interesting family. The mother was a very sweet lady who became president of the women's society in the Kintambo church. Her first daughter had never developed properly. She was a teenager when we knew them and had grown physically according to her age, but she just lay in a bed, could do no more for herself than a small baby. That mother fed and cared for her all those years. A younger daughter, Bernadette, was normal. Then there was a boy named Daudet (after the French author!). He became a friend to Jimmy, although he was several years older. He would take Jimmy to the market, where Jimmy wanted to buy a palm grub—not to eat, as the Congolese did, but to have for a pet. Failing that, he once adopted a rice worm, making a little Lego house for it. Then he wondered what to feed it!

We knew two African-American couples. That is, the husband was Congolese, the wife African-American. John taught at the seminary. He was one of three Congolese who had been sent to the States to study theology. Baptist women of California had paid for their wives to join them in the States, but his wife's family had not allowed her to come, and before long she died in the village. While in the States John met Anne and married her. She tried very hard to be a good Congolese wife. Probably the hardest part was adjusting to the idea that the whole extended family is welcome in your home for as long as they want to stay. One of their daughters was Jimmy's age, in first grade, but she was attending a local school. They came to our house one evening, and at my request she recited one of the fables of La Fontaine, her eyes glazing over in proper Congolese fashion as she quoted.

The other couple we knew less well. He was working in child evangelism. I think he was the one who told me about his baptism. He was in catechism class with other boys of his age, preparing to be baptized, when someone decided he was too young or for some reason should not be baptized at that time. He was devastated. His mother took him aside and asked, "Do you love Jesus? Is he your Savior?"

"Yes!" the boy protested.

"Then that's what counts. He's your Savior. You have him in your heart."

"When my friends were baptized," the man recounted, "I sat in the congregation and watched them, and it was all right. I knew I had Jesus in my heart."

The first year we lived in the Camp Babylone house, the rent was amazingly low—what a Congolese family would have been able to pay. The second year our landlord doubled the rent, but it was still very reasonable. The owners of the house moved back to Sona Bata and rented their side to a Belgian couple, then a Swiss one. When I invited the Swiss for a meal, I remembered that Europeans do not eat sweet with savory, so I refrained from glazing the ham—but it didn't occur to me that pineapple salad is sweet too!

In between tenants the other side of the house was empty. This worked out very well for us. Our friend Reuben had had a very sad college career. He was enrolled in science in the first year—he wanted to become a psychologist—when the President decided teachers were needed so badly in the far east of the country that they drafted university students to go out there and teach, whether they were trained or interested in education or not. They would then automatically be in the next year when they returned to college. Reuben was one of those who went. It was a very broadening experience, of course. He saw Stanleyville, which had been hit so hard by the rebellion, and people who had lived in the forest for many months. Then he was sent much farther east, where the people were not Bantu but Nilotic, and darker than Bantu. Reuben discovered he had prejudice against people who were darker than he!

Back in college, Reuben found that all those drafted teachers were now education majors, but that was not what he wanted. We suggested he apply to the rather new Protestant university in Stanleyville, which was looking for students. He did, and was accepted, but on getting there he discovered that they had too many enrolled in the sciences and he could only audit classes, not get credit for them. Reuben developed hepatitis, couldn't attend class anyway, returned. Now an uncle in the bush commissioned Reuben, back in Kinshasa, to buy a house and lot for him. After doing this Reuben realized that the same seller had sold the same lot to a couple of other people and he did not have clear title. The uncle was furious. Reuben's fiancée was unhappy because he wasn't writing her often enough, and Reuben's answer to that was to punish her by writing less often. We knew Reuben needed rest so he could recover, so we rented the other half of our house and invited him to stay there. He had meals with us. We learned a lot that year about the local culture and a little about witchcraft that we never would have known otherwise. Reuben wanted to know more about witchcraft but realized he couldn't find out all he wanted to know without getting involved himself. He read the New Testament through while he was with us. He told us, "I wish God hadn't given us free will."

Also during that time, Norm's folks came to visit. There was room for them, along with Reuben, in that other half house. They came by ship and brought a piano with them! At one time we played a duet, Mother on the piano and I on the harp. Later, after Norm's parents and Reuben had left and the Swiss couple lived in that side of the house, they finally told us, "It sounds as if the piano were right in the room with us." We moved it to the outside wall.

We had other pets in that house besides Spotty and her short-lived puppies. There was a darling white kitten the children named Snowsoft. One day we came home to find that boys from the next

Norm's parents joined the crowd rejoicing at the arrival of the piano

block had stoned her to death, just for the fun of it. We also had two parrots, one named Blue Eyes, the other, Puffin. One of them was in the house while we were playing Clue and bit the head off Professor Plum.

The third year the rent jumped from 16 zaïres a month to 100. We refused. At this time the Congo Protestant Council, for which Norm worked, was building new offices and associated two-family homes. He was invited to take one half house and accepted. The rent we had to pay was actually higher than the 100 zaïres we would have paid to stay in the Kintambo house. I prayed hard that we wouldn't have to move, but we did. A dedication date was set for the new buildings, and people rushed to finish them before that date. Most permanent houses in the Congo had concrete floors; they were often painted red or green. Ours were painted red. Unfortunately they were painted before the concrete had completely dried out. The result was that the paint never did dry. Norm ended up paying men to unpaint the floor, that, is, to scrape off the ill-fated paint. That done, we did move in. Electricity was not connected yet. Our first supper in the new house was eaten by the light of a flashlight stood upright in the middle of the table. Surprising how much light it gave!

One of Norm's roommates during his internship days (and nights) was now a successful allergist in Detroit. Allergies were a big problem in the Congo, and Norm invited Rudy to come for a visit and suggest ways to help. Rudy accepted. "As soon as I stepped off the plane," he reported to us, "I smelled mold." Rudy was particularly interested in training someone who could specialize in allergy prevention and treatment after he left. Norm did find a young nurse (male), who enjoyed learning about allergies. Then Norm took Rudy and nurse

Constantin to the Evangelical Medical Institute at Kimpese to speak to the students there. Later the three of them flew to a similar school at Tshikaji, in the south central part of the country, for the same purpose. They had various adventures. The government took their passports when they entered Tshikaji and didn't give them back till they were on their way to the airport to depart. In fact, they were so late that when they arrived at the terminal building there were only two boarding passes left for the three men. Rudy, being a man of action, extended his long legs over the counter and possessed himself of a third boarding pass. They boarded the plane with no difficulty.

The problem announced itself when they landed at an intermediate city. Passengers got off; others got on. Departure time came, but they couldn't depart because there was one more passenger than the number of seats! Our three men kept very quiet during the long delay. How the problem was solved they don't know, but they eventually arrived safely back in the capital.

Before Rudy left he told me, "You're spreading yourself too thin. You need to take care of your husband and children." He was right, of course. I rather abruptly turned my Sunday School teachers' classes back to Eva. She must have felt somewhat overwhelmed.

After the extensive surgery on his arm Norm had been prescribed sedatives. They got to be a habit. It's very easy for a doctor, especially in the Congo, to keep himself supplied with a prescription drug. Now we realized that Norm had become habituated to that sedative. It was no longer so effective, and he started taking it earlier and earlier so it would take effect by bedtime. Then he might half wake up in the night and act almost drunk with sleepiness. He didn't get free of that until our next furlough.

A pediatrician came from Sweden to help out in this needy country. She brought a brand-new Volvo. After a few months she became discouraged and decided to go home. She gave the Volvo to Norm and the Medical Department for his work. We then had two vehicles. Norm had hired a chauffeur who could drive around the city doing errands for him. Now they could go different places at the same time. One day Norm had our Volkswagen bug, so I took the Volvo to pick up our kids at the American School. It was my first time to drive a Volvo, and I felt very cautious. The road to the American School goes up a hill. It has one lane going each way with a middle lane for passing. The American School had begun on our American Baptist mission compound. Recently it had built new, larger quarters on the main route going south out of town. The entrance, on the left as you go up the hill, was not clearly visible from the highway. If you didn't know it was there, you might not realize there was a road going in.

So here I was, driving cautiously up the hill, looking in my rear-view mirror, signaling, moving cautiously into the passing lane. Once there, I stopped looking behind me, needing to watch for anything coming around the curve ahead. There was nothing, so I slowly turned to enter that inconspicuous road that led to the American School. When I had just about reached it, I realized there was an enormous government truck coming up on my left! Every lug in his front wheel made a little hole in my door. The driver, who had already lost his license, had assumed that I was moving over to pass a slower vehicle ahead of me, but I was too slow for him, so he planned to pass me in the far left lane.

I don't know how our kids got home from school that day. Someone in the government drove by and saw our two vehicles and realized what had happened, so we had a credible witness that it was the government driver's fault. The government would have paid for the repair to the Volvo, but it might have taken years. Our chauffeur knew someone in the bowels of the city who could repair our door cheaply, so we let Martin take the Volvo to him. When it came back, the door was repaired, but there was a new problem. Someone must have driven the Volvo in some pretty rugged terrain, because the front axle was bent, and there were telltale pieces of bark on it. Now the Volvo needed more repair. So much for not waiting for the government to act.

In 1969 Bob graduated from the American School of Kinshasa. Grace was two years behind him. She must have been about 15 when she received her first proposal of marriage. One of Bob's Congolese friends came to our home in Camp Babylone sometimes. One day he presented Grace with a poem he had written, in English: "Son of Africa, girl of America, can you be one?"

Grace responded mildly, "I'm too young to think about marriage." Come to think of it, she was a year older, and several years further along in school, than Reuben's Malia had been when they became engaged. No wonder the young man thought the time was ripe.

Both Bob and Grace participated in the excellent musicals the American School put on. The Class of '69, including a number of American Baptist boys, really shone. They produced *Oklahoma*—a very sad play, to my way of thinking, with great songs. Bob's good friend Glen played Curly, while Grace's friend's older sister, Anne, had the female lead. One of our American Baptist girls made a great Ido Annie, and John played the ill-fated Jud to perfection. Bob and Grace enjoyed being part of the chorus.

Let me not forget *Harvey*. Remember the friendly six-foot rabbit? Tim was offered the part of Elmer, Harvey's alcoholic but lovable friend. Tim didn't want it, and our Bob was the next choice. He did a fine job, and that activity gave just the boost he needed to his self-confidence. Many years have flowed under the bridge since then, but at a recent Congo reunion Bob entered the room holding the door for an invisible someone about his height and saying, "Come on in, Harvey. Do you remember these people?"

During Bob's senior year he dated an English girl named Juliet. I had read in Mencken's *The American Language* that there is more difference in speech from one English county to another than between standard British and American English. Hearing Juliet, I could believe it. Sometimes she could say a whole sentence without my understanding a single word.

It was probably during spring break that we went to the coast on vacation—our family of six, Cliff and Joy's family of six, and Juliet. Fortunately the vacation house was pretty well furnished at that time and included several bedrooms. Cliff and Joy had a bedroom, shared with their youngest child; so did we. A third bedroom housed the girls— Juliet, Grace, Linda, and Marjorie. That left the laundry room for Tim and Rick and Bob. It was not too comfortable. One day Juliet was going to make Banbury buns for us. I had brought food supplies from home, of course, and oh dear! I had put some soda in a baking powder tin. Juliet used it instead of baking powder, and though the Banbury buns tasted fine to us, she was understandably quite disappointed with her creation.

Graduation came, and Bob went back to the States to enroll at Kalamazoo College. He and Juliet had decided to go their separate ways; it would be difficult to carry on their relationship so far separated from each other, geographically and culturally as well. Our mission board gave each of our children in college one trip back to the field during his/her college years. Bob chose to take it the summer after his freshman year. A very responsible young man, he felt he could not come unless he could earn some money while in Congo, so I scouted around for him and found a job with an American construction company called Kalicak. Like many freshman students, Bob put on some weight during that year and arrived in Congo looking filled out and healthy. Then he went to work, doing the outdoor physical labor and also serving as an interpreter at times. Kalicak got a good deal when he hired Bob. He invited Bob to his home one time and gave him a shot of whisky—Bob's only taste of hard liquor ever, as far as I know. We were grateful that he got home safely. Those welcome pounds Bob had put on at college melted right away as he toughened his muscles and have never come back.

Bob had arranged to quit his job in time to have a couple of weeks for himself before going back to the States. He spent both weekends camping out at the rapids in the Congo River with his friend Ted, providing food for hungry mosquitoes. None of us thought about the fact that since we took our antimalarials on Sunday, Bob missed them both weeks.

Jimmy's birthday came in July, and his friends tended to be away. We had a tradition of inviting as many guests as the birthday child's years. We couldn't find seven boys that summer of 1970, so we had to invite girls. It turned out that, counting Jim, there were four boys and four girls. Thinking about it before the party, I remarked, "Isn't it interesting! All the boys are white, and all the girls are black."

Jimmy retorted with some indignation, "Blondine is not black. She's exactly the same color as Riaz."

He was right. Blondine was the daughter of the very black Congolese and the very fair African-American we told you about earlier. Riaz was Pakistani. (Why did I consider him white?) When they came to the party, sure enough, they were exactly the same color.

There were a lot of Pakistani businessmen in Kinshasa, and elsewhere in the country, and a number sent their children to the American School. A couple of Pakistani boys were in Marjorie's fourth grade. One day we were driving into the CBCO compound when Marjorie spotted two boys coming out and exclaimed, "I know them! They're Pakistaniels. Oh, no, that's some kind of dog, isn't it?"

CHAPTER FIFTEEN

Back to Sona Bata

Sona Bata needed a doctor. Norm was eager to get back to hospital work. But first he had to find a replacement as Medical Director of the Congo Protestant Council. He thought it should be a Congolese, and he thought of Marc, who had trained as a nurse at Sona Bata and worked there, then gone back to school for six years and graduated from high school and had the preparatory year for university. After that he went into education and worked as a school principal. He had training and experience in the medical field and in administration, and he was a committed Christian, honest and dependable, who worked well with others. Would he come?

Yes, he would! And he turned out to be very good in the job. He knew how to compromise and get along with others without sacrificing his principles. He was one of the finest persons we've ever known, and Norm's best friend in Congo. But it was a while before he could take over the work.

In 1970 we moved to Sona Bata, where Norm was the only doctor as before, with responsibility for hospital, nursing school, and outlying dispensaries, but now he had had polio and left the surgery to Tata Kimpiatu. Norm was there to give advice if needed. However, he didn't stay at Sona Bata all the time. He spent part of every week at the CPC office in Kinshasa, sleeping on a board he put across the bathtub. The building had been a private house before. After Marc came—affectionately called ya-Marc—Norm still made trips to the city to help him get broken in to the new job.

Bob had returned to the States. He visited my parents in Glens Falls, NY, and then Norm's. He felt unwell before he left them, but he went on to Eastern Baptist College to see his classmates Glen and Tim. While there he became really ill and was hospitalized at Bryn Mawr Hospital. Bob and his friends were sure he had malaria; then he remembered those mosquitoes at the rapids. But Stateside doctors do not believe in malaria until they see a positive smear, and people who have been taking antimalarials don't always show positive smears. Bob was in the hospital a week, unable to keep anything down, before treatment started. The second week he started to get well. Of course we didn't know any of this until it was all over. But something good, something very good, came out of it. The other students in Glen and Tim's prayer group found out about Bob, and some visited him in the hospital. One of the young women heard about this dreamy guy and decided she was not going to follow the crowd and visit him. Anna didn't meet him till he was out of the hospital and praying with the group before he headed back to Kalamazoo, now late to start his school year. But that prayer meeting started a relationship that culminated in their wedding two years later. Or should culmination include their children and grandchildren and ministry together?

As soon as the school year started, Grace went to the hostel. Marjorie and Jimmy were thrown into the local school with the Congolese children. "Jimmy," I had told him, "at Sona Bata you'll be going to school in French!"

At first he rather liked the idea. Later he changed his mind, telling his sister, "I won't go to the French school. Well (remembering the facts of life), I'll go if Mom makes me, but I won't learn anything!" I remembered that with delight when in third grade he came home and cut equilateral, right, and scalene triangles out of cardboard just because he wanted to. But first he had to get through second grade. It was the first of the grades to be taught in French. In the Sona Bata school they had used the local language, Kikongo, in the first grade. So French was new to all the second graders. Jimmy had an advantage in the fact that Mary was in his class. Mary's father was one of those three men who had been sent to California for further study, so she spoke English fluently and could give Jimmy a helping hand. At the end of the first semester the teacher reported that Jimmy, the missionary doctor's son, had passed everything except health and religion! He mastered those too by the end of the year.

It was during the following year that I asked him, "Jimmy, do you speak French with Mary? Do you speak Kikongo with her?"

Jimmy responded, "Mom, I speak all kinds of languages. I don't know what I speak!"

Another time we were in our bedroom when we heard Jimmy on the veranda with some friends. They had spotted an outdoor thermometer on the outside wall and asked Jimmy what it was. He didn't know the word for thermometer, so he explained in French, "It's something to tell the temperature." Yay, Jimmy!

Discipline was harsher than in the American School. Children sat at double desks. Once the teacher set out to slap Jimmy's seatmate's hand with a ruler, but the boy drew back his hand quickly and it was Jimmy who felt the ruler. Our children participated sometimes in punishment administered to the whole class. Each child had to bring a palm frond broom to school. Palm frond brooms are very effective. You strip off the frond until you have a thin, flexible fiber. When you have enough of these, you hold them together with an empty 2-oz. tomato paste can near one end. The fibers are springy enough to do a good job. It took a lot of palm fronds and a lot of work to produce enough fibers to really fill out the tomato paste can collar. Our children's brooms were always very skinny, and the collar had to be squeezed to hold the fibers in place.

One day the President was to pass by on the road outside Sona Bata, that went from the capital city to the seaport. The children learned rhythmic slogans and then marched out in their blue and white uniforms to stand by the road until the great man passed. Unfortunately he was delayed and they stood for hours in the hot sun.

Marjorie had a problem in school that Jimmy would never encounter. Her long blonde hair posed a great temptation to the boy seated behind her. He didn't try to dip it in the inkwell, but he did want to feel it. It was so different from his or his sister's. Marjorie got tired of having her hair handled, so she found a solution. She braided it and wound it around on top of her head. Yay, Marjorie!

Marjorie's friends included the children of the Dutch missionaries in a nearby house and Nzuzi, the daughter of the hospital chaplain who lived in the tiny house in between. One day Marjorie reported that the teacher had scolded her and Nzuzi for whispering. I rejoiced. Marjorie had become a normal student in a class where she was a minority of one. Years later, when Marjorie was in college, she visited Kimpese and saw Nzuzi again. Marjorie was way ahead in education but she was impressed with Nzuzi's experience in life.

At the end of the year Marjorie finished fourth grade with flying colors. She asked if she could skip fifth grade, since she had lost a year by repeating fourth because of the language barrier. Her wish was granted. She had no trouble with sixth grade. With this move she caught up with Florence, Mary's older sister. They became great friends. Florence eventually moved to the States and came to Marjorie's wedding.

One day in fourth grade she had come home stating, "The teacher says we have to have a new notebook, bought by our clean daddy." What's that? Oh, yes, the French adjective *propre* ordinarily means "clean," but not when it's put before the noun. The teacher had said, "Your own daddy must buy this notebook." I wonder who had bought the other notebooks.

I also gave the children some lessons in English at home. Another Dutch family lived at the other end of the station. They had spent some time in the States, and the mother wanted the boys to continue in English. She asked if I would teach them, and I accepted. In English school Marjorie was in fifth grade that year, Jimmy in second. The Dutch boys fit in between, in third and fourth. The principal of the American School in the city had offered to help us get materials from the States. The only trouble was that they were late in coming. What to do? Since I had taught Bob and Grace, there were books left from them. I found a reader at the right level for each child, and I must have found math books. For science, I had read somewhere that we should follow the children's interests. So I found some sort of reference book for each child. Jimmy's was The Little Golden Encyclopedia. When they suggested a topic, each one looked in his/her book to see if it said anything about that subject. Once we were in the middle of studying volcanos when one of the boys brought in a turtle. We dropped volcanos and studied turtles. However, since their teacher was much more interested in language than zoology, we mostly learned how to say "turtle" in four languages—English, French, Dutch, and Kikongo. We had a ball—until the proper books came. Then it was a scramble to try to catch up. One of the Dutch boys did not enjoy reading, and I wasn't flexible enough to make it easier for him. I finally threatened, "If you don't try harder I'm going to send you back to your mother." He called my bluff. I felt bad about that.

The local people very much wanted to expand the nursing school. Since there were only so many patients to work with and only so many nurses to teach the students, Norm didn't feel the school could grow very much without sacrificing quality. Other people didn't see it that way. It was important to educate as many young people as possible.

Every year we gave entrance exams to the applicants. I loved making up French and math exams, with questions designed to see if they could follow directions and think. Once I told them, "Draw a patient under the bed and a box on the bed"—partly to see if they understood the difference between under and over, and partly to see if they would follow directions that went contrary to what they would expect. In math I asked, "Which is greater, 132/144 of an orange or one orange?" But one time I did a very foolish thing. I had been working on entrance exams at my desk in our bedroom, and I had made an answer key. The next day we were taking a little trip, and I went away and left everything on my desk. Our house worker was very grateful that I had been so generous, enabling him to share the information with the applicants he knew—or maybe just one, who passed it on to others. We found out when correcting the exam papers because I had made one mistake in the answer key, and of course all those who had received the free help made the same mistake. We had a hard time explaining to the government official why we had to give a second entrance exam. We didn't punish our house worker. I suppose he and I should both have been locked up and fed bread and water.

One day a woman whom Norm had seen in prenatal clinic came to the hospital to have her baby. He had determined she would need a Caesarian section, but Tata Kimpiatu was away that day. Norm commissioned me to drive her some 36 kilometers down the road to the Catholic hospital. I felt uncomfortable about the situation and asked for someone who knew midwifery to accompany me. Fortunately one of our recent graduates was going that way and would be willing to be taken all the way to the hospital and then delivered to her destination on the way back. It would have made a good comedy scene: the woman in labor crying out with each contraction, her relative telling her, "Trust in God!", the nurse-midwife in front with me trying to calm them, and me driving and saying, "Breathe!", demonstrating panting there in the driver's seat. We arrived safely at the Catholic hospital, where the woman delivered naturally, without surgery.

In 1971 came the great name change. The President wanted "authenticity." The Belgian names of cities had already been replaced by African names. Leopoldville had become Kinshasa. The currency was already zaïres instead of francs. Now the President christened the country Zaïre. Our Dutch friends laughingly asked, "How would it be if the USA were called the Republic of the Dollar?" The President announced a competition to write the new national anthem.

In due time the winning song was chosen and published in the paper, complete with music. I sat at the piano and played it, and the children and I sang. And we laughed. Here we were, American and Dutch, lustily belting out, "We are Zaïrois!"

Grace graduated from what was now The American School of Kinshasa (TASOK), valedictorian of her class. She made her graduation dress. The night before graduation I was in her hostel room trying to help her. I wasn't too much help on the dress, which she was working on while memorizing her speech.

She chose Earlham College, although not because her Aunt Grace had gone there. She had two scary adventures that first year in college. Our sweet, pretty Rosebud had been a late bloomer socially. Her high school yearbook revealed that some boys had noticed her, but they had waited to write about it in the yearbook. In college that situation was rectified. She had all the dates she could handle. Once she naïvely told a young man, "I have the most beautiful view from my window! Come see." She was talking about the view from her dorm window. He interpreted the invitation differently.

The other adventure lasted longer. Grace got sick and figured she had malaria. She knew where to find the antimalarial we had given her for such a situation, but she didn't remember the directions for taking it. This powerful medicine was to be taken one pill a day for three days. She took all three at once. She wrote, "That weekend is just gone out of my life." Once again, by the time we heard about it the emergency was over. How good of God to take care of our children when we were far away!

As part of his college course, Bob worked one term of that sophomore year at St. David's, a camp for retarded children in the Philadelphia area, not far from the place where he had spent two weeks in the hospital with malaria. It never occurred to me at the time that he had chosen that opportunity to be near Anna. I was explaining to Marjorie and Jimmy, "Bob's at a camp for retarded children."

Jimmy asked innocently, "You mean big children like Bob?" I had to explain that Bob was working there, not one of the children. Now I understand that Anna was able to visit him there, both help and admire him as he played his guitar and led the kids in worship, and decide he would make a great daddy for her children.

I also had a scary adventure during that term. Remember our first term at Sona Bata? The 11 outside doors that we never locked unless we were to be away overnight? Times had changed. Now we locked all of them every night, but some weren't very secure.

One night we were in bed, but I wasn't asleep or at least not soundly, because I heard a man fumbling around on Norm's desk, beyond his side of the bed. I whispered to Norm. Of course the man heard me and left abruptly. He hadn't found the money he was looking for.

How did he get in? The dining room had French doors opening onto the veranda. I guess we didn't, or couldn't, lock the doors opening onto the veranda from the outside. The thief had entered the veranda and then pried out a pane from a French door so he could reach the latch from inside. Then he'd made his way through the dining room and living room to our bedroom, brave guy. He must have found Norm's little medical bag and carried it off with great glee, but when he saw it did not contain money he threw it down in disgust and we eventually retrieved it. Norm's reaction was to create a booby-trap of tin cans on top of our bedroom door. When one opened the door it would make a great racket and hopefully scare off the thief.

Some time later Norm was away on one of his many trips. A doctor who had occupied the house while we were elsewhere had converted half of the four-room cookhouse into an apartment for his mother-in-law. That made better accommodations for Marjorie and Jimmy than the veranda bedroom that had briefly been Kasavubu's. Between it and our bedroom were the breezeway and bathroom. I was reading in bed, by the light of a kerosene lamp, of course. For some reason I remembered that I had left laundry on the clothesline. So out I went in the dark in my nightgown and brought in the clothes. Perhaps it was the dog barking that had made me stop reading. Now I went back to bed. After a while the dog must have barked again. There was a window right beside the head of the bed. Outside, a man had pried up the window with a paring knife he had found in my kitchen. Through the opening were coming his hands and a gun. I jumped out of bed on the other side and dashed through the bathroom to the breezeway, picked up a pail and held it in front of my head, whatever good that would do, went outdoors and yelled at the top of my lungs in Kikongo, "Thief! Help me!" Later Jimmy, who had been back in the cookhouse apartment, told me, "I thought you were the girl thief yelling to the man thief to help her." Obviously he recognized my voice as female but not as his mother's.

No one shot me, and pretty soon men did come to help. The man who had come in through the window dashed out through the door to the living room, activating the booby-trap, of course. He also had the window drapery wrapped around him, unintentionally, I'm sure. The first helper was the very dark hospital chaplain, whose house was the closest. *"Tala! Mwifi!"* I yelled, mistaking my rescuer for the thief! Obviously I wasn't thinking very well. Sietzo, the Dutch missionary in the next house, set me straight. He found out that this was a group of men who had previously visited the Catholic station across the railroad tracks. One of the teachers (priests?) at their school had at some time flunked out one of the bandits, who this night had shot him. Then they had apparently decided to kill two birds with one stone and see what profits they could find at the Protestant center. We eventually heard that they were captured way down the road when their vehicle broke down. In the meantime Sietzo had arranged for one of the female nursing students to stay with me the rest of the night so this poor scared missionary would be able to sleep.

In the morning our cook heard the story and thought I was a pretty weak woman. He was right, of course. He explained, "I would have jammed the window down on his fingers. I wouldn't have screamed like a banshee."

Yes, Tata, you're a strong, capable man, and I'm a weak, bumbling woman. I would never have thought that I could succeed in imprisoning, or injuring, the man's fingers before he shot me. And there was a justification for the scream. I remembered the thieves who had visited our house in Kinshasa and then moved to the neighbors'. So I thought there was good reason to let other people know thieves were around.

You know the expression "afraid of your own shadow"? In the days— no, nights—following that adventure I found out what it means. After dark I'd hear the dog barking, look out the window and see someone moving on the veranda. It always turned out to be my shadow.

We had lived in the city three years. That meant there was only one year of our four-year term left for Sona Bata, but as that year drew near to a close there was no doctor on the horizon to replace Norm. There were plans to bring a Christian Indian doctor named Dhamaraj to another church center, if both governments and everything else cooperated. If he succeeded in coming, there might be another Indian doctor for Sona Bata. While we were thinking about this, Emmet and Eloys from California visited our station. They were an outstanding couple. We had been impressed by Emmet's prayer at an American Baptist Biennial a few years before. Now we asked him, "Will you pray that Dr. Dhamaraj will actually be able to come?" Emmet was happy to pray, and Dhamaraj did come—but no second Indian doctor for Sona Bata. Why hadn't I asked Emmet to pray for our own need? We lengthened our term by a fifth year.

Before we finally did leave on home assignment, the church center as usual had a good-by feast for us. There were the normal speeches, including somebody's words, probably in Kikongo, "We are very happy to say good-by to you." We interpreted that to mean that they were happy to give us this sendoff, not that they wanted to get rid of us. But maybe this time we were mistaken. That difference of opinion about expanding the nursing school loomed large in their thinking.

CHAPTER SIXTEEN

Highlights of a Furlough Year

Norm's work on a Master of Public Health degree at Harvard had not really accomplished anything, since he hadn't been able to take the first semester. Now, in 1972, he was going to do it right, at Johns Hopkins School of Public Health in Baltimore.

Where would we live? Just north of the city there was an institution called Koinonia Foundation (no relationship with Koinonia Farm in Georgia). It had been founded by Frank Laubach, Glenn Clark, and others to train people who were going abroad in any capacity—government, business, whatever—to share the gospel and to teach people to read. I had visited there for one weekend conference. They had been able to buy a 40-acre estate with lots of woods, a house big enough for conferences and several other useful buildings. People who came there for training had been blessed, but unfortunately not many actually went overseas after being trained. Koinonia had also started a literacy project in Sierra Leone. After some time they were in financial difficulty keeping up their extensive property in Baltimore and also the project in Sierra Leone. They decided to change the nature of Koinonia and make it a place where primarily college students came for an alternative semester. A young Episcopal priest became the director. He had a lovely wife and a toddler. A few of the "old Koinonians" stayed on. Dick, an older man, and Helen, whose youngest daughter was there too, reveled in organic gardening. Another woman was in charge of the housekeeping, a big responsibility with the various dwellings, meals for everybody, all the details. An African-American couple ran the large kitchen, but Dick made the oatmeal from steel-cut oats, which cooked quietly all night on the back of the large range. He also made whole wheat bread, in which he might put whole peanuts, pieces of carrot, a host of delightful surprises. Unfortunately our son Jimmy did not share my appreciation of that healthful bread from which I made his sandwiches every day. Eventually he confessed, "I lick off the peanut butter and throw away the bread."

"All right, Jimmy," I sighed, "from now on I'll make your sandwiches from 'cotton batting' bread."

Before coming to the States I had written to ask whether we could live at Koinonia for that year of study. Norm wouldn't be able to do a lot in the life of Koinonia, but I would. Their reply told me about the change in Koinonia but said we would be welcome to come, so we did. It was indeed a change. Things were very informal and free. Anyone who had anything to share was welcome to share it. I taught a little conversational French class for a few interested people. Once a man came who made and played hammered dulcimers. A woman from a church brought an art technique that initially stimulated a good deal of interest. The second week she came the enthusiasm had somehow leaked out. She commented, "Yes, it's very fluid here. It flows, and it ebbs." The students must have enjoyed their alternative semester, typified by the multicolor candlesticks they created by letting candles of different colors melt down the holders. The next semester they presumably went back to college. I wonder what effect Koinonia had on them. Any spiritual input would have been very low-key and due to the Christian personality and lifestyle of committed individuals.

I helped can the enormous tomatoes that came from Dick's garden. We even harvested green tomatoes toward the end of the season, and I shared my mother's idea of green tomato mincemeat. In the spring I worked in the garden a little, weeding strawberries. Strawberries are difficult to weed, because another plant looks very much like a strawberry plant before the blossoms come out. I mistakenly dug up more than one strawberry plant—but there were still a lot to freeze when harvest time came.

We had an apartment in a two-story building. Just above us lived a young public health doctor and his wife, a charming couple. They taught a class based on the book *I'm OK, You're OK.* The doctor was also helping some people to quit smoking. One young fellow was coming along well until McGovern (remember presidential candidate George McGovern?) was so soundly defeated. Then he turned back to his comfort habit.

We discovered an Episcopal church that knew about the gifts of the Holy Spirit and had healing services. One of our friends at Koinonia, one of the few older people like us, came to a service with us. She was amazed to see the church parking lot full on a weekday evening. "This is an Episcopal church?" she exclaimed. It was good to go there. I'll never sing "Walking and Leaping and Praising God" without remembering that powerful little church.

Our own church was in Towson, across the north side of Baltimore from Pikesville, the address of Koinonia. Down in the city there were some black and white churches, which we would have enjoyed, but they were down in the city, too far to drive. The Baptist Church in Towson was dually aligned American and Southern Baptist. Marjorie got to be a queen in Acteens. (Every girl became a queen if she fulfilled the requirements.) While we were there they started putting people together in home groups. We really shared from the heart and grew spiritually and bonded with the others in the group. We learned about the Church of the Savior in Washington, DC, where each member of the church was involved in some ministry. Here in Towson a group of women studied a book *The Eighth Day of Creation,* written by a member of that church. She encouraged us to look for gifts God had given us, try something new.

With that impetus, when the school was looking for den mothers for Cub Scouts, I decided to see whether that was one of my gifts. (It wasn't.)

The town of Pikesville was a golden ghetto, inhabited largely by well-to-do Jewish people. At the meeting, none of the Jewish mothers volunteered to mother a den, only another Gentile mother and I. Neither of us had any experience in the field. She lived in the country and had horses the boys could get acquainted with. I went to all the meetings for den mothers and tried to do what we were supposed to do. KISMIF was the slogan: Keep It Simple; Make It Fun. I tried but did not succeed. These boys were so sophisticated, and Jimmy and I were so clueless. I came to the conclusion that what the boys really wanted was not a Cub den but a basketball team. I think they all had basketball hoops attached to their garages. Poor Jimmy did not play basketball. Once I brought them out to Koinonia, where Jimmy was in his element, because he knew how to climb trees. It was the style that year for boys to wear their hair long. Our neighbor the public health doctor caught sight of my Cubs and commented afterward, "I never expected to see so many little Jesuses." But unfortunately I kept the boys too long that day. It was Friday, and they needed to be home before the Sabbath began. I should have been aware of that. As it was, one mother phoned me and explained the problem. I was very apologetic.

Another unforgettable adventure with the Cub Scouts: We were doing something connected with music, and these fourth-graders were way beyond a rhythm band. One boy brought his violin. The Koinonia director's wife offered, "You can take my Volkswagen to pick up the boys and take them home." For the trip home I opened the hood, in front of course on a Volkswagen, to put the violin in. On the freeway the hood popped open; I hadn't fastened it properly. No, the violin didn't fall out, but the hood stood in front of the windshield and I couldn't see where we were going. I was able to pull off and stop, no damage done, just a scare. My friend did not offer to lend me her car again—nor did I ask.

This was Jimmy's first year in the States since he was three, Marjorie's since first grade. They adapted pretty well. Jimmy got demoted to a lower math group (!) after the first marking period. The next section was on the metric system, and Jimmy had used that exclusively in Congo, so his grades went up considerably. Marjorie sang in the junior high chorus. We attended their Christmas program. The director, an African-American man dressed in striking red and black, had chosen a number of real, Christian Christmas songs, which those Jewish children sang and their Jewish parents listened to with pleasure. I visited Marjorie's school one day. She loved her English teacher. The social studies teacher managed her class superbly but with a good deal of sarcasm. She kept the boys in the back of the room busy but never called on our daughter on the rare occasions when her hand went up. I'm afraid I was mean. At the end of class I said to the teacher, "You know that blonde girl on the front row? Her name is Marjorie."

After those years in the tropics, the children were really looking forward to winter and snow. Someone lent them a saucer for sliding downhill. One late fall afternoon while we were raking leaves, it started to snow, and before nightfall the ground was covered. In the morning the snow was still there, and the kids looked forward to saucering after school. Alas! The sun came out and melted all the snow during the day. And all that winter it never snowed where we were. It snowed north of us; it snowed south of us; it snowed west of us; it snowed east of us, over the ocean, but not on Baltimore. At Christmas we went north to my parents' in New York State, and the kids enjoyed snow at least a foot deep, but no chance to use their saucer on the exciting hills at Koinonia. Spring came, and one afternoon snow covered the ground. The kids were wise by now and got up early the next morning to take advantage of the snow before school. They slid down the slope that was pretty bare of trees a number of times, then decided to try the side with more trees. Pretty soon Marjorie came to the door crying. "I don't know what day it is!" Her head had run into a tree; she must have suffered a slight concussion. Whatever day it was, a social studies test was scheduled. We figured if she didn't know what day it was she probably wouldn't remember the exports of Brazil; we kept her home that day. Some well-meaning soul lent her a fiendish jigsaw puzzle—round, with all sorts of candies jostling each other. What a choice for someone with a concussion!

Norm loved his Public Health course at Johns Hopkins. The profs were great. One of them, about Norm's age, invited the class to his home, where they got to know each other socially. Some of his fellow students came from countries where they might go back to be the Minister of Health. Norm made plans for a Health Zone centered at Sona Bata. The hospital would be the nucleus, overseeing the dispensaries Norm had supervised, which would be converted to Health Centers, with emphasis on wellness and preventive medicine—nutrition, immunizations, checkups—not just dispensing the proper medicines to treat diseases. The third layer—really the first one—envisioned a Mama Bongisa in each village. *Bongisa* means "improve, make better." A Mama Bongisa is a mature, respected woman who strives to make her village a better, healthier place to live. She encourages parents to see that their children get nutritious food every day, especially the little ones who have just been weaned. Traditionally the father gets the best food, the mother second best, and if there's any left the children can eat too. Mama Bongisa keeps track of pregnant women and sees that they get prenatal exams. If there are indications that the delivery may be complicated, she makes sure the expectant mother plans to arrive at the hospital before labor starts. She's aware of illness and accidents in the village, encourages immunization and sends people to the Health Center when they need to go.

Is Mama Bongisa remunerated? Yes, in the village way. She's already looked up to; now she becomes everybody's grandmother. She has her own gardens, with manioc and corn and peanuts, but if they didn't flourish, the other women would help supply what was lacking. A man might give her an especially delicious papaya from his tree or a stalk of bananas. If the village is near a stream, a big fish would find its way to Mama Bongisa's from time to time, and anyone who was able to kill a monkey or an antelope would make sure Mama Bongisa got a choice portion.

CHAPTER SEVENTEEN

Our Longest Home

At Johns Hopkins Norm had planned a Health Zone centered at Sona Bata. Now it was 1973, time to return to Congo and put that plan into action—but Sona Bata did not want Dr. Abell back. It wanted to triple the size of its nursing school, and Dr. Abell wouldn't cooperate.

Well, who did want him? IME, *l'Institut Médical Évangélique de Kimpese* (the Protestant Medical Institute of Kimpese)—the medical center Dr. Freas had tried to direct us to all those years ago. Norm would be their first full-time Public Health doctor.

Accordingly we moved to Kimpese, to the rambling house we would occupy for ten years, longer than either of us had ever lived in one house before. Actually, we would have two five-year terms there, with a year of home assignment in between.

IME was laid out in separate pavilions, all one-story—a medical pavilion, a surgical pavilion, obstetrics, pediatrics, and orthopedics, because one of the founding doctors had been an orthopedist. They even made artificial limbs there, excellent ones. A mile or so away stood Kivuvu (Place of Hope), a leprosarium. Few patients lived there any longer, because contemporary treatment allowed leprosy patients to go home and live in their villages. Those who did remain had suffered a good deal of damage before the new medicines became available, but they were able to do some useful things. For instance, they grew vegetables and sold them. People had finally accepted the fact that they would not catch leprosy by eating vegetables that leprosy patients had cultivated.

We found many Angolans living and working in the area. In fact, the man who came to be our cook was Angolan. Also some British and Canadian missionaries who served at IME had previously worked in Angola. How come?

The country of Angola borders the Congo on the south. Angola was for centuries a colony of Portugal. In 1961, when almost all the other countries of Africa had achieved independence, restless groups in Angola began guerrilla warfare against the Portuguese government. That war continued until 1975, when Angola finally became independent. During those years many Angolans had come north, fleeing the Portuguese, and had more or less integrated into society in the Congo, although Congolese tended to discriminate against them. Now when Angola was newly independent, some went back. The church at IME had a fine Angolan pastor, and another Angolan pastor lived at CECO, the mission station that trained teachers and pastors, on the other side of town. These men were among those who returned, and they asked Norm if he would help them plan the church's medical work in the newly independent country. So Norm made five trips to Angola to work with them. Marjorie and Jimmy and I accompanied him on two of the trips. On one our cook went with us. We would be driving by an area where all we could see was grass, and he would say, "There used to be a village here."

"How can you tell?" we wondered. If you'd lived in a village like that, I suppose you'd know.

We saw that the roads were all dirt, but well-kept, rolled dirt roads. The Portuguese government had done well on that. Dirt roads in Congo were not that good; the Belgians had relied on villagers with hoes to keep the roads in condition.

Once we all slept on bamboo mats on the concrete floor of a classroom. I think that's the only time we ever did that. It was hard, but we slept. How touched we were to see two old people reunited after being separated by years of war! Of course we tried to learn a little Portuguese. One of those pastors explained, "The Portuguese use their nostrils a lot." Angolan Kikongo—think of the Queen's English in comparison to American speech—differed from the kind we used in Congo, and also, where our Kikongo was liberally larded with French words, Angolan Kikongo naturally incorporated Portuguese vocabulary.

We visited the ancient cemetery where the Kongo kings were buried—vertically, in cylindrical tombs rising up above the ground! These are the ones we'd read about in African history. One of the kings became a Christian and sent his son to Portugal to be educated. He came back a bishop.

In 1975 the Portuguese transferred the government to a coalition of the three Angolan political parties that had been fighting for independence. Unfortunately, the coalition did not last. Just when the church in Angola was getting organized for medical work, and other things, of course, war broke out again, with three armies fighting each other. Instead of Norm's going over to help the Angolans, the Angolans came to us.

The village of Songololo, with a striking church and a thriving dispensary, numbered some 5,000 people. In one day its population tripled with the arrival of refugees from Angola. The first agency on the scene was Doctors Without Borders. They organized relief efforts, food, emergency medical care. Norm worked with them, of course.

And some of his first Village Health Zones were established in the refugee camps that soon got organized.

Norm supplies Angolan nurses with medicines

Refugees kept coming. Some arrived at the hospital at IME. Life in the villages in Angola had become very difficult. One army would descend on the village and demand their help, their food, etc. Naturally, with guns threatening them, the villagers gave it. When that army had passed through, the army that was fighting them would come and burn the village because they had aided the first army. So people fled to the forest and lived on palm nuts. Some who arrived at IME were wearing cloth made from bark. It worked, but it didn't last very long. And some died of starvation, with only grass in their stomachs. An Angolan family of five came in desperate condition. One missionary took the seven-year-old boy into her home to try to nourish him back to health. Another took the baby. The boy didn't make it, but the baby recovered, was adopted by a Congolese pastor and wife, and grew to be a fine young man.

A Congolese woman went with Norm to the refugee camps and talked to the women about the Christian family. "The wife is the driver," she explained, "and the husband is the mechanic." She discussed nutrition and encouraged them to grow manioc (the staple food) and become self-sufficient.

One of the Angolan women stood up and said, "We want to, but how can we?" holding up a manioc root attacked by blight. Another problem. We came to feel that the biggest medical problem was not malaria, not any other tropical disease, but malnutrition.

In addition to the hospital, IME included a school for nurses. These were called A2. A1 nurses corresponded to RNs in the States. A2s had a high school education, plus one year. They came to us after ninth grade and received four more years of instruction, mostly nursing subjects but some French, math, science, and history, with English optional. There was also a section for laboratory technicians. Helen had come to the field to train lab techs, but through the years she'd had to work as a nurse instead. Now at last there was a lab school where she could use her special knowledge. She was a very special person, too. Whenever she encountered someone, she would ask herself, "What does God see in this person?" or "What does God want me to do for this person?" One student was found to be drinking. She could have just put him out of the school. Instead she said to him, "If you have a drinking problem, we can help you."

During the years, I taught various subjects at that school, in both the nursing and lab sections. French was my responsibility in the lab school that first year, until we got a Frenchwoman who had taught in Canada before coming to the Congo. That first lab class was quite small, about twelve students, and only two girls. Several of the students had completed high school but had been unable to go on to the university, so they came here as a career option. One young man traveled all the way from the province of Kasai, where, he reported, all you had to do to pay your school fees was dig up a diamond. Another had completed the philosophy section and knew a lot but could not condense what he had to say. The girls suffered in comparison with those who had completed several more years of school. One day we were reading a selection entitled *"Les Vers du Roi."* I asked if they had any questions, and one girl raised her hand. "What don't you understand?" I queried.

Honestly she responded, "What it's all about!"

Now it happened to be about verses, poetry. It seems Louis XIV enjoyed writing poetry. The word *vers,* however, can also mean "worms," so I asked these lab students, "Is it about intestinal worms?"

"No." They knew better than that.

The word *verre* means "glass;" "Is that it?"

"No." That wasn't where the trouble lay. Actually, why should Congolese lab techs be reading about the machinations of a 17th century French king? I tried to find something more appropriate and less flowery for them and discovered a book by a French journalist that had to do with medical or paramedical problems. One chapter dealt with defoliants used in the Vietnam War. Remember Agent Orange? The writer said that it had been used *à grande échelle.* That means on a large scale, *échelle* being the word used on maps in "a scale of 1:500," for example. But the more common meaning of *échelle* is "ladder," so the other girl quite naturally envisioned our soldiers in Vietnam climbing a very tall ladder to apply Agent Orange to each tree. Isn't language confusing!

One part of the curriculum required the students to study Shakespeare (!)—in French. Shakespeare in French? Well, a Frenchman named Anouilh had translated four of Shakespeare's plays into excellent French, and our nursing school had the book in its library! Anouilh reported that it had been very hard work, much harder than writing a play himself, but what a good job he had done! I considered it as fine as Shakespeare himself. I chose "Twelfth Night" for my little class. After reading it, we picked out a few scenes that we could perform with a cast of twelve, including only two women. The countess and her mischievous maid were portrayed by females, but the heroine was played by a young man who resembled—in size and shape and color, anyway—the one who played her twin brother. Since the heroine (played by a male in our version, and in Shakespeare's theater, for that matter) disguises herself as a young man in all the scenes we showed, it was confusing for the audience, but they loved it, especially the sword fighting between two people neither of whom wanted to fight. Our philosophy major drove me up the wall by not memorizing his lines until the last minute, but he had them down pat at the performance.

I also taught history to the nursing students. I used to give them a five-minute quiz at the beginning of each period, based on the previous lesson or the reading assignment. Then I realized that they were forgetting earlier work and I needed to review. So one day, without warning them, I asked them questions like "Name a country of eastern Europe," because we were going back to eastern Europe, although we had just finished a lesson or two about the exploration of the Pacific. Students in the Congo, and I'm sure they're not alone in this, tend to keep their noses in their notebooks until the very last minute before a test. One girl reluctantly closed her notebook as she came into the classroom, took out her pen and wrote. Her country of Eastern Europe was the Bering Strait. I was reminded of geography class one of those very first years at Sona Bata, where we had studied a map of Africa and the then Belgian Congo, after which I rolled up the map and asked my students to draw Africa and the Congo. At least one girl had a rather large glob for Africa and a smaller glob out in the ocean for the Congo.

In the second semester, the final class in history took up general problems, the first being world hunger. I presented the first problem; teams of students presented the others. One bright boy, captain of his team, took the floor wearing a pair of glasses he had made, using them to read his notes and taking them off to look at the class, just as his teacher did with her glasses. That class came at 2:00 p.m., right after our precious siesta. At least once I went off without my glasses, and my dear husband, who was at that time director of the school, presented himself, and the glasses, at my classroom door.

Part of our study was African history, including those kings whose tombs I eventually visited, as well as other kingdoms that became part of the Belgian Congo. The first year I taught that, I discovered that the kids knew their original ancestors had been hunters, fishermen, and gatherers, and they knew the current president was Mobutu Sese Seko. Everything between was a blank. So the next year I took pains to teach about Diego Cão, the Portuguese explorer who discovered The River (Congo, later Zaïre) 10 years before Columbus arrived at Hispaniola. Then I told them about Livingstone and Stanley, who in searching for Livingstone got bitten by the exploration bug and ended up traveling the length of the Congo River, which he thought at first might be the Nile. On the final exam I reaped this delightful response: "In 1482 Diego Cão discovered The River. Four hundred years later Stanley went looking for him, and he found him!" Now to be fair, I'm not sure that's what the student meant. The same pronoun in French means "him" or "it." It may be she was saying that Stanley went looking for the river. That's considerably closer to the truth.

I taught an elective English course to nursing students, without much success. They tended to think that because the course was elective, attendance and homework were also elective. One day I had come across a little song used in Sunday School with the English-speaking children: "If anyone asks you who I am, tell them I'm a child of God." I thought, "My English students should be able to understand that." I tried it on a couple of them one day. They didn't get it. Finally I translated it for them.

"Oh, shield!" one of them exclaimed. That's how you might pronounce c-h-i-l-d if it were a French word.

"But that's not English," I explained.

"It's our English," she countered.

She had failed to turn in some important homework in history class and didn't do very well on the final exam, so she flunked. The director of the school, one of our other missionary doctors that year, asked me if I could regrade her exam so she passed, as history was the only subject she had failed. I found that I could look at her paper from another angle and pass her. The next year she failed anyway, not just history.

My most successful English class was the one I taught lab students. That's because it had a very narrow objective—to enable them to understand the English on things they used, such as labels and instructions for reagents. This was a brand-new school; Helen was making up the curriculum and courses. She asked me to create the one for English. I took the basic lessons she was teaching in French and put them into simplified English, limiting the new vocabulary introduced in each lesson. Most medical words are cognates, so it's pretty easy. I took a hint from my high school English teacher and had the kids write each new word in their notebook with a definition and a sentence. The first lesson was on the microscope and its parts. They had no trouble until they came to the microscope stage. How do you define it without talking about microscope slides? I hadn't introduced that word. The French word for a microscope slide is *lame*. It usually means "blade," so most of them talked about putting a blade on the microscope stage, but one smart fellow had a feeling that wasn't right, so he looked around for another translation of *lame*. Aha! It also means an ocean wave, so he put waves on his microscope stage. Well, they learned lab English pretty well. They couldn't say a correct sentence in English; one boy presented himself at the office saying, "I am come for to take the chalk." The assistant director figured out his English teacher needed chalk. But one of our graduates came back and told me that the doctor he worked under depended on him to read English.

I also taught religion. It was called Bible, but I thought it included more than that. The Old Testament in modern French was in process of translation. A partial edition of the Old Testament had come out that just touched the high points. I thought that would be ideal for the brief overview I had time to give them. They knew about creation, but after that they were very vague, so we started with Abraham. I tried to apply the Scriptures to their own lives. "Think of something very precious in your own life, something God gave you. Would you be willing to give it up if God asked you to (as Abraham was willing to give up his precious son)?"

One day I happened to tell another class about Frank Laubach's "game with minutes," how he tried to relate to God every minute of the day. I have tried at times to do that but never come anywhere near. One boy in that class was named Madituka. He was not an outstanding student, sort of average, a little bit of a clown. That young man became the leader of the local Scripture Union, probably the most vibrant and growing Christian organization in the country at that time. He was chosen with one other to attend the Hospital Christian Fellowship, an organization for nurses that then existed in Africa only in English-speaking countries. The meeting was held in Malawi. Madituka and his companion enjoyed meeting black and white nurses from South Africa who got along with each other. They were invited to visit Soweto on their way back to the Congo and miraculously were able to get visas and go there. Madituka came back and started organizing Hospital Christian Fellowship at Kimpese and then in the whole Congo. Now he's the national co-coordinator and the trainer for all of Francophone Africa. He married one of his classmates, and that couple bears an amazing Christian witness, tried in the fire of personal tragedy. One day long ago, when Madituka had become leader of the Scripture Union in the region, some of us were asking, "How did you get this way?"

He replied, "One day Mme Abell told us about the 'game with minutes.'" That boy I hadn't paid much attention to had put it into practice. Later I realized his parents must have been deeply committed Christians; he had a solid foundation.

Madituka and Fwauna, with God's guidance and the power of the Holy Spirit, produced four fine sons. They were especially proud of, and grateful for, the first-born, Patrice, who became a doctor. By this time the family was living in Kinshasa, so it was easy for Patrice to attend classes at the University. For his internship he went to IME, Kimpese, his parents' alma mater. At church in the city, his mother missed seeing and hearing her son play the piano as he always did, but God whispered to her, "He's where he belongs."

Later she found out the deeper meaning of that message. That Sunday afternoon, enjoying the freedom of the weekend, Patrice and some friends went to a small waterfall on the hill behind Kimpese, where we all enjoyed swimming. The young men would dive from a rock at the top of the waterfall and then swim in the pool below. They were about to go home when Patrice called out, "One more dive." He dove. He did not come up. Others dived in to find him. There was no trace of him. Eventually, horrorstruck, they returned to IME to tell the appalling news. By then it was dark. The next day a professional diver searched for Patrice. Still nothing.

If there was ever ground for believing in witchcraft, surely this was the case. How else could a full-grown, healthy man dive into a pool where people dived all the time and just completely disappear? His parents did not succumb to the temptation. They did pray, "Lord, give us back our Patou!"

Madituka went to Kimpese. Finally the body did float to the surface. Somehow it must have been caught under a layer of rock. They had planned to take the body to Kinshasa for burial, but it was in no condition to be taken, so it was buried at IME. Fwauna came from the city with her other sons. Now when someone dies in the Congo, people wail. If they have come some distance to the funeral, or to the wake, they don't wail all the time during the journey, but when they arrive and meet the other mourners they start wailing again. Fwauna stepped out of that car singing a hymn. God had repeated to her, "He's where he belongs."

The bereaved couple eventually wrote a book about Patrice, his life and death and life. They called it *La Rose Remise à sa Place* (The Rose Put Back Where It Belongs). We would probably not compare a man to a flower, but in African thinking that's all right. I've never known anyone whose faith and trust surpassed theirs.

Another opportunity came when Helen offered me a class called *séminaire*. It was far from a college seminar, but it was a discussion group, and I could choose what we would discuss. Wow! I realized that I wanted them to take notes, and the first thing I needed to do was teach them how to study. I remembered that when I started college we were given a little booklet telling us how to study, which I found very useful. The traditional way to study in the Congo is to copy in one's notebook whatever the teacher writes on the blackboard and try to memorize it. I wanted them to listen and understand and write down what they thought was important, whether it was on the board or not. I gave them math problems with extraneous information included, to try to get them to sort out what was necessary. I wanted them to think, and they found that difficult.

After that I started basing our discussion on books by Walter Trobisch, a German missionary to the Cameroun. Starting out in education, he came to specialize in marriage and family. His most famous book is called in English *I Loved a Girl*. The translation doesn't quite render what the French says. In French the tense makes a difference. The perfect tense, used in this title, indicates a one-time action, e.g., "I made love to a girl." Loving her over a period of time would be expressed by the imperfect tense. It's the thought-provoking story of a young man who is fired from his teaching position by the church because of adultery. He writes to his mentor, Trobisch, and

Trobisch replies. In a series of letters, the young man brings up one argument after another to justify himself, and Trobisch teaches him, letter by letter. Finally Trobisch sends his young friend a ticket to come see him, and the young man opens up and confesses deeply, is forgiven and starts home a new person. On the bus going home he meets a girl whom he sees with different eyes. They fall in love, and the sequel talks about their problems, as the girl's uncle wants her to marry someone else. After that book we went on to another and another of Trobisch's, and the students identified with his characters. This led to useful discussions. One of the girls said, "I'm a serious girl (not free and easy)," and I'm sure she was sincere.

The boys answered her, "Then pay attention to what you wear." I don't think she had ever thought about the relationship of the length of her skirt to how boys thought about her.

On another subject, the students told me about the bribery and corruption rampant in the country. "Little people," they explained, "are used to being gouged. They've finally realized they can gouge others too. They're seeing clearly now."

"It's possible," I tried to convince them, "to see even more clearly, to understand what happens in the long run when everybody gouges everybody else." It's hard to think of the long run when your children are hungry. We did hear about a group of Christians who had vowed neither to offer bribes nor to accept them. That takes a great deal of courage and faith. Missionaries don't always follow their own principles.

In our later years at Kimpese, Norm gave me responsibility for the cold chain. All the village health zones and dispensaries gave vaccinations. We had a supply of cold boxes in which we packed the vaccines with ice to send out to the villages. Vaccines that got warm could not be depended on.

∞

We didn't see much cholera, but at one time we heard of some cases in the area. The hospital made preparations for any cases that might come to us—cholera beds in a special room and extra precautions to prevent its spreading to other patients. Then one day Norm came home saying, "Well, we have our first case of cholera."

"Oh, my. So they're using the cholera room." The patient was a habitual drunkard who was employed by the Catholic sisters of another mission in town. Unfortunately the staff on duty was so excited by the event that they forgot to put him in the room prepared for such patients. The hospital was crowded, and a woman waiting to deliver was ensconced on the floor in the corridor where the cholera patient waited. She contracted the disease. The man recovered; she did not. I learned that cholera can be successfully treated simply by giving rehydration fluids (water with a little bit of sugar and a tiny bit of salt) persistently, every few minutes. But it's much faster if you have the right antibiotic. We saw no more cases of cholera.

Great excitement at IME! Then Vice-President George H. W. Bush was visiting Kinshasa, the capital (called Leopoldville before the great name switch), and Barbara Bush was going to come down-country by plane and visit IME. Such preparations! In the Public Health Department, the posters about nutrition and hygiene and disease prevention were all translated into English. The English versions would not be useful after Mrs. Bush's visit, of course, but there they were. People from the Bushes' entourage came to prepare our staff. They practiced what they would do, down to the minute. Someone was to present the lady with flowers; they had to be inspected first. Everyone lined up on the sidewalk between pavilions as they would to greet Mrs. Bush. Well, almost everyone. A surgical operation was in progress. The petite missionary doctor and her patient remained in the operating room, but the nurses and the anesthetist obeyed the higher priority of getting ready for the big event.

On the anticipated day the weather did not cooperate, the flight did not take place, and Mrs. Bush never saw Kimpese.

That was a very minor incident compared with what occurred at the time of the famous Mohammed Ali versus George Foreman prize fight that was held in Kinshasa in 1974. The Department of Tourism, if there was such a thing, felt sure that many Americans would travel to Zaïre for the great occasion, and plans were made for tourists to come to Kimpese. Behind the town and the mission stations the Bangu raised its lofty head. It's not a mountain, just a deeply eroded plateau. It took us white adults about an hour to climb it; the local boys scrambled up in fifteen minutes. A stream called the Vampa tumbled down in two waterfalls; below each one a pool invited swimmers. Yes, that's where, years later, Patrice would drown. To get there we had to drive through town to the other Protestant center and through it to a manioc field where we found a swaying wooden bridge across the stream. On the other side of that we hiked through a mango grove and other foliage to reach the lower pool. But in preparation for the droves of tourists expected to come for the boxing match, a parking lot large enough for several buses had been carved out of the manioc field and a solid bridge built, held up by enormous tree trunks and wide enough for a car to drive across. Of course there was no road on the other side. In the mango grove slim tree trunks made benches in case folk wanted to stop and have a picnic. Then a little wooden bridge had been built so one could cross over to the other side of the Vampa without wading. To our knowledge nary a tourist used the parking lot, the bridge, or the benches. Eventually the small bridge was taken by somebody for firewood.

There were enough missionary kids at IME to justify a small school. The year we came there, Florny taught first through fifth grade. A young British missionary taught kindergarten. Florny was an experienced teacher in the States and had previously volunteered as an extra houseparent at our hostel in the city. She organized those children so that each one did his own work at his desk. When he needed her he would put up a little flag, and she would come to him as soon as she could. (Of course some were girls, but he/she is so cumbersome.) There were educational games in the back of the room to be used when regular work was done. The younger children came early in the morning, the older ones maybe an hour and a half later. Then the older ones stayed later. This gave Florny a chance to work with the two groups separately. Visiting her classroom, I exclaimed, "Florny, this is amazing! Every child is working at his own pace; no one's goofing off or disturbing the others. How do you do it?"

She said, "It took me six weeks to get everything working smoothly," but once she did, it was amazing.

In addition to all the classwork, and reading to the children every day—I think she read *The Hobbit*—she put on "The Wizard of Oz." Lanky Jimmy played the scarecrow. Arthur was the cowardly lion. A Swedish missionary who had become sort of an aunt to his family made his costume. It was fun to see him running around before the performance asking, "Where are my paws? Where are my paws?" The tin woodsman did fine in rehearsal, but just before the performance he was struck by stage fright and vomited all over the yellow brick road. Fortunately it was made of leaves and could easily be swept away and replaced. Replacing the actor was something else again; as luck would have it the MAF boy who played Dorothy's uncle was able to take over the role. Of course he had to use a script, and that posed a problem because tin arms don't bend at the elbow. But the performance was a delight.

The IME faculty was composed of missionaries from the UK, the US, Canada, Norway, and Sweden, also that one French teacher who wasn't a missionary. And they represented different denominations. One was the Evangelical and Missionary Alliance. They had a policy that missionary wives were not to homeschool their children; children had to be sent away to school. One such couple lived in Boma, well on the way to the coast. They sent their daughter to the English language school in Kinshasa for a year, but it was very hard on all of them, as it took them two days by road to make the trip there. They asked if they could send the girl and her brother, now six, to our little MK school at Kimpese. They would have to live with one of our families. I thought it might be a good opportunity for Jimmy, who had always been the last child of the family, to have someone younger to look after. Marjorie was now living at the hostel in Kinshasa. Everyone agreed, and the two children moved in. They were very nice children. The girl was 10, very easy to deal with but homesick. The boy was a fine lad but a typical six-year-old boy. Jimmy, 11, was not used to rooming with a little brother. It wasn't always easy.

Our second year at IME Florny was gone, and a sixth grade was needed. The English missionary took first grade along with kindergarten, and a young American missionary wife was invited to teach the other five grades. Unfortunately, she developed a serious disease and had to leave the country. We resident missionaries divided up the various subjects. Annabelle, a single missionary, taught science; MAF wife Evie took math and read novels to the children. I was responsible for social studies and English. One day two fourth-grade girls came to my desk for help. They were studying adjectives. They'd been given a list of nouns and were to think of two adjectives to go with each noun. They were doing well until they came to "grandmother." "All we can think of is old," they complained.

"Well, I'm a grandmother," I informed them, a bit proudly. I was in my late 40's. "Am I old?"

"Ah, middle-aged grandmother!" What else?

Later I thought I should have asked, "Do you have two grandmothers? How are they different?"

But they might have answered something like, "One lives in California and the other in Tennessee."

As you know, I loved directing Christmas pageants. I always liked to include Simeon. One of our committed nursing students was playing Simeon, but he made people laugh at his trembling gait. I told the fellow, "You're *pretending* to be an old man. *Be* old." He was able to do it.

Another year I tried to reproduce a Christmas pageant Agnes Sanford described in one of her books. She probably would not have recognized it. Our fine Dr. Mwimba had a great baritone voice and agreed to sing an appropriate hymn to begin the drama. To my surprise he sang one stanza only. Afterward I asked him, "Why didn't you sing the rest of the song?"

He explained, "I was kept at the hospital and had to run to the church to get there in time. I had just enough breath for one stanza!" How wonderful of him to make it in the midst of his busy doctor's life!

The pageant included some lighting changes, which I managed simply by turning on or off the switch at the back of the sanctuary. However, as the pageant progressed, more and more people crowded in, and sometimes someone's back would change the lighting inadvertently. Afterward one of my students asked me, "Was that you playing with the lights?"

That was such a beautiful little church. Once an African-American tour group visited Kimpese. When they entered the church, they spontaneously sat down and worshiped.

Directly across the road from us lived the Mpia family—father, mother, and three children. Relatives criticized them because there weren't more children coming along. Mr. Mpia taught math, but his heart was in music. Now if I want to learn a new hymn or song, I play it on the piano and then sing along with it. Mr. Mpia would sing it from the notes; then he could play it. He had named his firstborn Mozart,

Beautiful church at IME

and the boy was living up to his expectations. The year we went to the States on home assignment I left my little Irish harp with the Mpias. Mr. Mpia's fingers weren't quite slender enough to manage the strings easily, but his four-year-old daughter found she could pick out a favorite song on the harp. After we came back and the harp was back at our house, we invited the Mpias over for an evening. The little girl tried to play the harp, but oh dear! I had tuned it to a different key, and it didn't sound right at all. Many years later when visiting a Congolese church in the US, I was amused to be introduced as "the woman who taught Mozart to play the piano"!

It was Mr. Mpia who told us about the charismatic group that met in the next town. The church there had been founded through the efforts of British Baptists, but some of its members came from the Manianga, the area that had been evangelized by Swedes. When Simon Kimbangu had been preaching and healing in that area, these people's parents had discovered the gifts of the Holy Spirit, and their descendants, biological or spiritual, continued to operate in them. Kimbangu was so popular that the Belgian government, and perhaps the British Baptist mission, considered him a threat. Apparently the Swedish missionaries and the church they founded were not troubled by the remarkable healing that characterized Kimbangu's ministry.

Tata Butedi, the leader of this present group, told us, "When times were hard, when we were being persecuted, we heard the Holy Spirit speaking to us more often." These people were now leaders in the local church, which did not appreciate their charismatic form of worship, so they attended the traditional church service in the morning, and were loyal workers in the church. Then in the afternoon they met in another place to worship in their own way. At first that would have been in or outside someone's home, but by the time we visited them they had built their own small building.

We enjoyed worshiping with them and trying to conform. Everyone took off any jewelry and removed pens from pockets, also shed shoes. There was a small room at one end of the building where people could confess to one of the leaders before the service started. There were no pews or chairs; the men stood on one side of the room; the women mostly sat on the floor on the other side. All the leaders were men, but all the prophets were women. If one of the prophets had a message from the Lord, she would go on her knees (because that's the way Manianga women did) to one of the leaders, who would bend down and listen to her. A woman on her knees can have dignity and be respected and listened to.

Every woman had one or two rattles. Some are made of gourds with seeds inside; others are metal with pebbles. On the men's side were drums and a metal instrument that was hit like a gong. I found the noise deafening until I learned to get inside it.

At one point in the service, while singing was going on, individuals would go one by one to the end of the room opposite the leader and then dance the length of the room to the leader, who would grab the person's hand. I think you might call it testing the spirits. I tried to do it too, but I never felt comfortable or thought that it was accomplishing what it should. It was just a form for me. (Norm never tried.) One day I was explaining this to one of the women, and she asked me, "Don't you ever dream that you're dancing down the room to be tested?"

"No, Mama, I never have."

These people practiced healing and casting out evil spirits. They were for real. One of the women lived at IME; her husband worked there. A person from another village who belonged to the same charismatic fellowship entered our hospital with no family member there to take care of him. Our IME friend would leave her own work to come and help that unrelated person. She had not been to school; she said God had taught her to read, that she could read only the Bible. I observed that she could read the hymnbook too; probably she could read print but not cursive writing. Congolese teachers use cursive writing from day one, so kids who go to school learn that. When this woman had a baby, she named her after me. What were my responsibilities? Treat her like my own self! I'm afraid I didn't do that. I think we had moved on by the time "Mama Abell" was ready for school, otherwise I would have paid her school fees. I should have kept in contact and fulfilled that responsibility no matter where I was.

There were failures and disappointments. Norm trained a young nurse to oversee the Rural Health Zones, replenish their stocks of medicine and advise the rural nurses. The young man learned and did his job well. He became a personal friend and even invited us to his traditional wedding. We had attended a number of church weddings during our years in Congo, in villages and in the city. They were similar to the weddings we knew in the States, with a few differences. We were surprised at the first wedding we attended, at a village near Sona Bata.

The officiant asked, "Who gives this woman to be married to this man?"

Two men stood up. "I, her father, do," announced one of them.

The other man then added, "I, her mother, do." What??

The officiant then asked, "Who gives this man to be married to this woman?"

Two other men stood up. "I, his father, do."

And "I, his mother, do."

We were invited to a colleague's wedding

Eventually we understood that in the Bakongo culture it's more important to know which side of the family a person is on than the gender of the person. Your mother and all her siblings are your mothers. If you want to be specific you have to say "the mother who bore me." Likewise, your father and all his siblings are your fathers. Yes, you can have male mothers and female fathers!

We had never attended a traditional wedding. I was under the impression that it would consist mostly of drinking and dancing. This one, at least, was not like that. The father of our friend the bridegroom took a mason's trowel and pretended to be laying stones or bricks or concrete blocks to make a wall. As he did that he chanted, "I'm building, building . . ."

Then the bride's father did something similar. He too chanted, "I'm building, building . . ." They were symbolizing the promise of each family to support the new family that was coming into being with this marriage.

But after some years Norm heard rumors that his *protégé* was prospering dishonestly from his responsibilities. Eventually Norm had incontrovertible evidence and had to let this leader go and train someone else. It was a heavy blow.

Another young graduate disappointed us. As a student he had been the one to go with Madituka to the conference in Malawi. On graduating he was hired by IME, but before long he was let go. There was some question as to what had actually happened, and we thought he was innocent. Our dear friend Marc, heading up the Medical Department of the Church of Christ in Zaïre, asked us to recommend someone to assist him, and we recommended this young man. It turned out we had been wrong; the IME authorities had been right.

Then there was a student in our nursing school who developed mental problems. We knew and esteemed his mother, and I prayed hard and tried to help the fellow, but to no avail.

Another student developed glaucoma shortly after beginning the nursing course. Although he was at a quality hospital—albeit we didn't have an ophthalmologist—and received the best treatment known there, his glaucoma developed very fast and he had to drop out of school.

The school had a good library. How it came to boast a French translation of Shakespeare I have no idea, but it had a large number of books spanning a good deal of the Dewey Decimal System. It also had a bunch of novels translated from English into French and donated to schools in the Congo. Someone meant well, but the selection of books was impressively inappropriate. I read one. At the end the immoral protagonist gets what he deserves, but how many of our students would read it to the end? In the meantime, we would certainly not want them to follow his example or to base his picture of Americans on that book. I quietly disposed of it. Unfortunately I was not the only one who took books from the library and did not return them. It was very difficult to keep a French-English dictionary in the library—too valuable, too tempting.

The years went by. Jimmy had been in fifth grade our first year there. We wanted him to keep up his Kikongo and French and have Congolese (*Zaïrois*) friends as he had had at Sona Bata, so we sent him over to the other side of Kimpese, to CECO, the Pastors' and Teachers' School, where there was a good primary school for the local children. He could go with Zaïrois kids from IME and have the first two classes there, then come back to the English-language school with the upper-grade MKs (missionary kids) from CECO. This worked well until exam time. The main subjects, French and math, were always taught first thing in the morning. However, there were extra hours of French and math at other times, and of course Jimmy missed those. On the exam he got a question about something he hadn't studied and answered it by writing, in French of course, "Why must I know about that?" To Jimmy's embarrassment the teacher thought that so funny he read it to the whole class. At that point we decided Jimmy could stay on our side of the tracks for his schooling.

In March of his fifth grade Jimmy made his decision for Christ. It took him a while; when he decided, he decided with his whole heart. The good Angolan pastor you've heard about let Jimmy study the catechism booklet by himself. I guess Jimmy didn't understand how well he needed to know it, because when the pastor questioned him he flunked and had to study the book again. After passing the test, he gave his testimony in church, in French, including the words, "I don't want to sin any more." And he was baptized in the baptismal pool behind the church. A few days later I asked him to get something at the local market. He pleaded, "Please don't send me to the market. The kids tease me, 'So you don't want to sin any more!'" (Though sincere in that initial decision to follow Jesus, he emphasizes now how much of a process it is—requiring repeated decisions to obey Him, day by day.)

Teasing was hard for Jimmy to take when he went to the hostel in Kinshasa too. Especially during his first year there, other children found that it was easy to get a reaction from him. We shuddered to think what would happen if another boy broke Jim's model plane with the 6' wing span. That did not happen. One of his roommates was David, a couple of years older, who became a good and lasting friend. And during his hostel years Jim matured until as a senior he was a boy that younger kids went to for help and counsel.

In 1978 Marjorie graduated from TASOK (The American School of Kinshasa) and we all went back to the States on furlough. Marjorie didn't go with us but with her friend Betty. We had neglected to do something connected with her passport or visa or vaccinations and it was touch and go for a bit as to whether she would be allowed on the plane, but she was.

Our son Bob and his wife gave us the Ungame. It looked like a game. It included a board, dice to throw and "men" to move and cards to draw. It was actually a device for getting people to talk and listen to each other. Almost everyone enjoyed playing it. We had fun with other missionaries and with Congolese too, and we learned some things about their culture. One of the questions on the cards was, "What was your favorite birthday present?"

Birthday present? Not in the culture.

"What's the most important quality of a mother?"

"Hospitality." That important! It was a long time before we realized that we should never let anyone leave our house without at least offering something to drink.

I remember the evening we played the Ungame with three or four interns from the medical school in Kinshasa. Their education included a lot of theory but little hands-on experience. So in their last year they were sent out to hospitals where they could get that experience, and IME was one of those hospitals. I like to think it was one of the best. These men were very intelligent, of course. They knew English, so they could read the cards in the Ungame. One of them drew the question, "If you could find the cure for one disease, what one would it be?" That intern was not the sharpest of the group, but he did seem to be the most dedicated and caring. The disease he chose was malaria.

One of the others questioned his choice. "Why didn't you choose something like cancer?"

The first man pointed out, "Malaria affects so many people. It takes so much time away from work. It weakens you. It really takes a huge toll on society." It was that young doctor who came back after graduation to work at IME and actually took over the Public Health work when we went on furlough in 1978.

That last week before our departure was pretty hectic—not so much for me. School was out, and I could devote all my energy to packing up. I do remember leaving a partly packed suitcase outside our bedroom on the screened back porch and finding some things missing before I finally closed it. But in general I was able to keep to my plan of packing up one room a day. The last room was our bedroom, which also served as Norm's home office. The rest of the room got packed, but Norm stayed at the hospital, preparing the new doctor to take over his work, until afternoon of the day we had to travel to the city and make our plane. When he came home, great activity, sorting papers, throwing some away and packing others in the right places. We became less exacting as the time flew by, until finally we were just tossing papers into foot lockers. Jim helped by toting the full containers to the attic of the house next door, where we were allowed to store them during our absence. Fellow missionary Charlie came to take us to Kinshasa and joined in the frantic filling, closing, and toting. At last we were off. Then when we got to the city, Norm had to stop and transact some final business with Marc, who had taken his place at the medical department of the Church of Christ in Zaïre. We did make the plane on time, and Charlie survived the stress of trying to pry us loose. Finally relaxing on the plane, Jim felt in his pocket and found the key to the staircase that led to the next-door attic. We mailed it back from Brussels, but of course the neighbors needed to get into that attic long before the key reached them.

There were three American Baptist churches in Kalamazoo. First Baptist kept close connections with Kalamazoo College; that was where Bob and Anna had been married. It was naturally the most intellectual of the three churches. Bethlehem Baptist was more conservative, with a number of people from the South. A third church was the most active in social justice. We attended Bethlehem because it had the most for our young people. But we parents went to Sunday School at First Baptist and occasionally our family attended the third church on special occasions.

My parents were living in a retirement community in Florida. When they first moved there they had kept their old house in New York State so we could have it to retire to, but after a year they realized 1) that it's not smart to hang on to a house when you're too far away to look after it, and 2) that we would probably not want to retire in New York State, with our children far away and no other reason to live there. So they sold the house, and in 1979, Norm and Jim went down to Florida and helped my parents choose a house for us only ten miles from where they lived.

Then came our second five years in Kimpese. Doctors from Doctors Without Borders had lived in our house while we were gone, and taken good care of it.

On our last home assignment, 1984–1985, we lived in that house in Florida, the only time we ever owned a house. It was good to be there; my dad died during that year, and Mother stayed with us while he was in the hospital.

CHAPTER EIGHTEEN

Our Children Spread Their Wings

Jimmy had a little difficulty adjusting to life at Kimpese. There were other MKs (missionary kids) his own age, but he wasn't fully one of the group at first. At one point I decided to give him his first driving lesson in order to add something positive to his life. Norm was away. He didn't itinerate like earlier, evangelistic missionaries, but he did seem to be away at several crucial times. Well, for some reason I took Jimmy over to the agricultural station (yet another mission station at Kimpese!) for our practice. He remembers very clearly backing into a palm tree. Before we left Kimpese he had developed into a very skillful driver. Come to think of it, by then he was in college.

After furlough, in the fall of 1973, we had arrived back in Zaïre just in time for school to start; we'd sort of dumped Marjorie at the hostel, and she never saw her new home till the first break, probably Thanksgiving time. That was tough. The first year, in eighth grade, she roomed with her old friend from Moanza and Kinshasa, Linda.

Everybody thought it was a good idea—Marjorie, Linda, both their parents, the hostel mother. It didn't turn out that way. They were too much alike; they ended up staying in their room a lot. They both enjoyed being with Marie and were each jealous of the other with her. They both did much better later with other roommates.

When Marjorie was 14 she and Mark became very interested in each other. Mark's parents were both doctors, Mennonites, working at Kimpese—very capable people, good friends to us. Mark was slightly older than Marjorie and had a sister slightly younger. Then there were Arthur, a classmate of Jimmy's, and seven-year-old Robby. Once I remarked to the girl, "All four of you are so smart, it doesn't seem fair!"

She replied, "But if one of us weren't, think how bad he'd feel!"

IME was administered by an outstanding Congolese man named Mandiangu. Our houses were diagonally across the road from each other. He had a son the same age as Jimmy and Arthur, who played with them and knew quite a bit of English. One day I asked one of the boys to give back a book by Munro Leaf that I had lent him. When he appeared with it, I showed it to the boys. The subject was prehistoric man, but the book began by talking about ancestors—grandparents, great-grandparents, etc. For some reason I told them, "Jimmy's great-great-great-great (26 greats)-grandfather was King John of England." Then honesty impelled me to admit, "He was probably the worst king England ever had."

Little Robby was tagging along with the bigger boys. At this he piped up, "I sure hope Mark doesn't marry Marjorie. We wouldn't want anything like that in our family."

Well, he didn't. They eventually broke up, but they remained friends all through high school. When the students put on "Our Town," Marjorie played Mark's mother—and made the wedding gown for his bride. Mark headed up the photographic staff of the yearbook his senior year. The yearbook was sent to the States for printing. It arrived back in Zaïre in time for graduation, but Mark was deeply disappointed in the quality of the photos he had worked so hard on.

He wrote in Marjorie's copy, "This book should be glued shut with the printers inside." The next year, Marjorie edited the yearbook. The staff decided to have the printing done locally.

Marjorie was a project person. At home in the dry season vacation, she might stay up all night working on a skirt for me, something for herself. Late at night in her room was a good time for a mother-daughter talk.

The first event of our year of home assignment in 1978 was Grace's wedding. She was marrying Michael, a graduate student at Western Michigan University (WMU). They were buying a house, which Grace was already living in, but they had a right to a college apartment, so they lived at the college and let the four of us have their house for the year. Bob was at WMU too; the whole family lived in Kalamazoo that year. Marjorie wanted to work for a year before she started college. She got a job at a doughnut shop, then a taco place. Jim took his sophomore year at the local high school. That fall, he initially worked for an eccentric old guy who sold and repaired bicycles, also all sorts of other things that only he could find. He promised Jim that he would teach him to spoke a bicycle wheel if he worked well, but the promise was never kept. After snowfalls made his bicycle commute to and from that job impractical, Jim made a little money delivering a weekly advertising paper. That job was also difficult until the snows had melted.

Before returning to the field we saw Marjorie enrolled at WMU. On the parents' orientation tour we found that at the noon meal she could have her choice of 30 different foods and 20 different beverages. She told us later that the food was great except that they turned off the orange juice machine at 11:00 a.m. Marjorie had said she would enjoy rooming with someone from another country; they gave her an Iranian roommate. She was in what she persistently called a four-man suite. One of the other two girls became her roommate the next year.

In 1981 it was Jim's turn to graduate from TASOK. Earlier that year he and Gary had climbed the cliff at the coast and inscribed on it in large letters "Class of '81." Jim was valedictorian of his class, as Grace had been. Foreseeing that, I had encouraged Jim to take public speaking. He followed my advice and did himself proud at graduation.

Marv and Bob, MAF pilots at Kimpese, had given Jim his first flight lessons at IME. Jim found it wasn't as thrilling to be actually flying a plane, as straight and level as possible, as making a model one soar and dip! But he did want to be a pilot, and eventually he decided that yes, he did want to be a missionary. He followed David (his good friend at the hostel) to LeTourneau College, which was tops in training mechanics. An MAF pilot had to be a mechanic too. When Jim graduated from LeTourneau, John, our first MAF pilot in Congo, was marshal of the graduation procession!

It was during that second term at Kimpese that Bob and family came to visit us. Bob was in his final year of med school and was able to take one of his clerkships in the Congo, at our hospital at Kimpese. Bob and Anna now had four children. Anna let me homeschool Kiesi and Theresa. Tim had reached the inquisitive age of two, and Serenity was just learning to talk. I played ball with her, singing, "Roll the ball" as I sent it between her legs.

She didn't learn the whole sentence, but it was a thrill to hear her say, "Baw."

Someone must have come around with a chameleon for sale. Bob bought it, and his big girls had a great time with Sam, ugly as he was. Anna did not like him so well.

One day Anna saw a mouse. She did just what a woman is supposed to do—she jumped up on the dining room table.

Jim had had an encounter with a mouse some time before. He opened his desk drawer, and a mouse looked up at him. He quickly shut the drawer, and while we were at the Sunday evening picnic at the guest house, he enlisted aid in getting the mouse. We looked for a cat. Someone offered an adolescent kitten, not guaranteeing it would be a mouser. Two Dutch boys came over. So, after the picnic, three tall high school boys, one tall man, one medium woman, and one small cat came into Jim's room and shut the door. The kitten headed for the window, but Jim was sure he knew where the mouse was. He opened the drawer—and naturally the mouse had left the same way it had entered. So where was it? The kitten had been right; the mouse was hiding between the curtain and the window. But by now a very intimidated little cat was hiding under the bed. Not so the mouse. It amazed us by its athletic feats, leaping to the top of the chest of drawers

Bob and Anna's family visiting Congo ... what a joy for us!

and then to the top of a picture on the wall. But none of the large humans in the room could catch it. Finally everyone left but Jim. He kept it for several days and then inadvertently crushed it in the door trying to keep it from escaping.

While Bob's family was there they lived in our house. Our neighbors, two single ladies, were going to be away, so they let us stay in their house. They had a dog and advised us, "Just go in as if you belong there." We did and had no trouble. Later we learned that that dog had occasionally bitten a stranger. Just as well we didn't know that at first.

When the clerkship was finished, Bob and family and I went down to the coast for a week. Norm wasn't able to get away. Tim took all his Little People (tiny wooden figures) with him. Next door there was a boy maybe seven years old who took the time to play with Tim. The beach house had a porch in the back, high off the ground as it sloped down toward the water. Tim's new friend helped him fish off the porch, making a fishing pole for him and tying a rock to the line for Tim to pull up. Tim loved his rockfish and took it back to Kimpese with him. Much later, back in the States, we were all looking at photos taken on that trip and were amazed to see how many Little People had gone on vacation with Tim. The number was much reduced when we left the beach house. But Tim was delighted with his rockfish.

Bob's last excursion in Congo was to be a trip way up-country to Vanga to show Anna   where he had lived and to observe the hospital there. They were set to start out one morning, but the vehicle wouldn't budge; it was dead as a doornail. Both knowledgeable men, father and son, exerted their brains to find the problem. Garage staff was called in. Finally, after some hours, it was discovered that little Tim had found a bolt and stuck it in an inviting slot which turned out to be the cigarette lighter. That was what had happened to the battery. The departure was delayed till the next day.

After two years at Western Michigan, Marjorie had transferred to Oral Roberts University, where Bob was in Medical School. ORU did a wonderful job of preparing students for summer mission trips. After her sophomore year she went with a group to Burkina Faso (formerly Upper Volta), and the next summer she led a group of five to the Congo. We met them at the airport and brought them to Kimpese, where Marjorie stayed with us, the other young woman lived with a Congolese family, and the young men went to the leprosarium a mile away and made their home with missionaries there. The first evening they were there, the group visited the Scripture Union and prayed for the leaders. Later they participated in a youth retreat. The other young woman declined the fish heads that supplied the protein for one meal.

The ORU students had several other opportunities to talk to groups and to pray with people. At one point the young women went to the other station (where Jim had gone to French school) and the fellows stayed with us. Then two of the men went up on the Bangu and

ORU Summer Missions team, in the home of a pastor and his wife

itinerated with the pastor there. When they came back from a grueling hike to another village, Rory looked at the hill on which the pastor lived and thought, "I can never walk up that." So he ran!

All three fellows had secured international drivers' licenses, but none of them had had experience with a stick shift, so Marjorie and Jim, who was visiting that summer, did the driving. After several weeks with us, the team traveled to Kinshasa for ministry there. Marjorie learned to be decisive and confident through that experience. When they arrived at the airport to go back via Paris to the States, one fellow's name was missing from the passenger list. Marjorie had re-confirmed all of them at the right time, but somehow he had slipped through the cracks. Marjorie stuck to her guns, and finally the agent gave them the five boarding passes they needed.

Jim stayed on a few more weeks. When we took him to Kinshasa for his flight back to the States, there was a letter from Marjorie. We read it on the way to the airport. Rory, the student on her team who was the most gung-ho about using French, the one she considered her co-captain, had told her on the plane to Paris, where he was staying for his junior year abroad, that she meant a lot to him and he wished she was coming to Paris too. Marjorie had had no idea. Pairing off was forbidden during summer mission, as it would break up the team. Marjorie had already done her junior year, and you can't take your senior year abroad. Now she wrote, "I won't do it if you don't want me to, but everything has fallen into place for me to take a second junior year in Paris." We had the rest of the trip to the airport to decide what we would write to Marjorie.

While Jim waited for his flight to be called, I wrote something to the effect of, "Wow! Well, it looks as if God is arranging this for you. Follow his guidance, and God bless you." And before we retired from the Congo we made a trip to the States to attend Marjorie and Rory's wedding.

CHAPTER NINETEEN

Kikongo Is Not So Bad

When we first arrived in the Congo in 1956, there were eight American Baptist mission stations, four down-country (downriver from the capital) and four up-country (east of the capital, in the interior). We were assigned first to Sona Bata, later to Kinshasa and eventually to Kimpese, a union station with several denominations working together. The one down-country station we never lived at was Nsona Mpangu, the successor to Banza Manteke, our oldest station. The up-country posts included Kikongo, Moanza, Vanga, and Boko. Norm made surgical visits to Boko from Sona Bata, and once the children and I went with him. (Grace remembers sleeping in a crib at Boko, even though she was seven years old, because it was screened in to protect her from mosquitoes. She also remembers the delight of being offered her choice from several individually packaged cold cereals, her first time ever! At home we ate oatmeal.) We had three short stints at Moanza and two years at Vanga. Now in 1985 Norm was invited to join a Congolese doctor in starting Public Health work at the Kikongo hospital.

I had never wanted to go to Kikongo. I'd heard that people there were ornery, and I had a theory that it was because it didn't cool off there, even at night. However, Kikongo had changed. Our dear friends Cliff and Joy, whom we'd worked with at Moanza, had gone there to direct the pastors' school, and I think Joy in particular had been able to unite the women so there was no longer unfriendly rivalry between the pastors' school and the rest of the station. It was easy to see how the station people would be jealous. Pastoral students, although poor as church mice, got a lot of attention from missionaries. The wives were trained as well as the husbands; there was even a three-year kindergarten for their children.

In 1985 we went to Kikongo and spent some happy years there. There was no house for us, so Pierre-François built one. It took a while, longer than expected; Cliff and Joy invited us to live with them until our little house was completed.

Pierre-François? Where did he come from? Well, he came from France, as you might think from his name. His father had vineyards there; P-F had gone to college and become an architect, but now he was at loose ends and didn't know what to do with himself. He would have liked to go to Canada but didn't have the money. So he hitchhiked to Zaïre! He must have flown or gone by ship across the Mediterranean, but from North Africa on he made his way by land, arriving finally in the capital city of Kinshasa, where an architect and his wife whom P-F knew were living. He turned up at their door one day, and they welcomed him.

Mrs. Müller was attending Bible studies led by a dynamic Swiss missionary named Jacques Vernaud. She took Pierre-François with her. It changed his life. I asked him once, "Pif, did you grow up in the Catholic church? Did you have faith as a child?"

He replied, "Anything I had had was all gone by the time I came here." Now in this strange city he gave his life to Christ. Here comes a confession. We had heard of this Swiss missionary and privately thought of him as a sheep stealer. That is, some members from our churches were leaving to join his church. When we came to know Jacques Vernaud and his delightful Dutch wife, we realized that church members were changing churches because they hadn't found dynamic, life-changing faith in their old church and they did find it in his. Instead of feeling jealous, we should be learning from him.

Mr. Müller put Pierre-François in touch with John, our American Baptist builder stationed at Vanga. P-F told us about the promise the Lord had made to him in a vision. He saw misty light and heard God assure him, "You've left your parents, but I'm giving you new parents." Jacques Vernaud became his spiritual father. Then when he arrived at Vanga one morning at dawn, mist was rising from the river—his vision! And at Vanga Miriam, Dr. Dan's wife and a gifted, dynamic, deeply committed missionary nurse and teacher of nurses, became his spiritual mother.

Now John sent the young Frenchman to Kikongo to supervise building there. P-F testified once, "When I accepted Christ, he changed some things in my life right away. I stopped drinking and womanizing. Later on I learned other things, like how to treat my workers." We found him a delight to know and a stimulus to our faith and practice.

Pierre Francois in a Congolese home

During his time at Kikongo he met a Canadian Mennonite missionary and traveled quite a distance by motorcycle to visit her at her station. Their backgrounds were very different; P-F reported they "had a lot of brush to clear away." One thing they had in common: both their fathers had vineyards! They eventually married and settled down in Canada, where P-F continued architectural work and they raised a family of boys.

The house Pierre-François built contained interesting contrasts. There was no hot running water, of course, but the enclosure around the bathtub was made of mahogany. It did turn out that there was a nest of snakes inside that enclosure, but that got taken care of. Kikongo was hot, as we had heard. I wrote one day that the temperature in our bedroom was 96 degrees, although it was only 90 in the living room. I was consulted about the color of paint and indulged my fancy in deciding what color I would like for each room. It turned out they would all be the same color, probably cream. It was a good little, two-bedroom house—little by our standards, big to a Congolese. Once at another station a visitor from America, speaking from the pulpit, said he had been born in a little five-room house. In Congo those two terms are contradictory.

In all our years in the country our cook had usually been a man, but now we had a mature woman as cook. She was a good worker. Once when we had bought a fish someone had caught in the river, she asked, "Can I have the head?"

"Why, yes, Mama, sure you can have the head." When she cut off the head it seemed to me that fish's neck must have extended well down into its chest.

"That's a really large head, Mama."

She replied, "No, it's small," meaning that her portion was definitely smaller than the part of the fish left for us. That was true.

Her teen-age son had frequent, heavy nosebleeds. She talked about buying a guinea pig so he could drink the blood. Unfortunately, we never found out the cause of his hemorrhages, and he eventually died.

The pastoral students were all married. A few of the wives had a high school education, with some teacher training. Some came not knowing how to read. The rest fell somewhere in between. It must have been a challenge to plan a program so that each woman could receive education appropriate to her needs. Joy and her staff accomplished that. Then, because their mothers were in class, the children had to be taken care of too. School age boys and girls went to the local school with the children of doctors, nurses, professors, workmen, all the other folk on the station. For the three- to five-year-olds Joy ran a kindergarten. Now that I was there and wanting to teach, Joy asked if I would teach an experimental first grade for those who had just graduated from her kindergarten, to see how they would do in comparison with the other local children who had not had the benefit of kindergarten.

Never having taught first grade, except for my own children, I jumped at the chance. I limited myself to what the other first grade teachers had—a textbook for the teacher, none for the children. A blackboard and chalk. In our early years in the country, first graders used slates and slate pencils. Now they used little notebooks. What a waste! The six- or seven-year-olds scribbled in their notebooks, thinking they were copying what the teacher wrote on the blackboard. I went back to slates. I furnished the slates; all the kids' parents had to buy was the slate pencils. If they didn't even do that, I'm afraid I provided them. I made experience charts; writing on large sheets of paper something the class had done or talked about, or a simplified version of the Bible story we were studying. I don't know where I found the paper for that or the easel. I also did something the local teachers never would have had the time to do. Every day I took home all the slates and put an exercise on each slate for the child to do the following day. I used ideas from American workbooks and adapted them to Kituba, the language the children were learning to read and write. The lessons, handed down by the government, used the Laubach method, with a picture for each letter sound. The first week we learned the vowels. "A" was represented by an open mouth in profile, saying "ah." If you work at it, you can make that mouth into the letter "a," which in Kituba says "ah." Learning vowels was frustrating because vowels by themselves have no meaning. The second week we used a woman's breasts (clothed) to illustrate "m," and we learned the word *mama,* like the English word but including any woman. Since we had studied all the vowels, we could then learn *meme,* which means "sheep," and so on.

Teaching reading was great fun. As they learned a new letter, the kids started writing it, both in manuscript and in cursive, because from second grade on they would be copying their teacher's cursive writing.

One day during the first week of school I was heading for a house I hadn't been to before, looking at the way ahead, not at the ground underneath my feet. I came to a little drop-off and managed to chip an ankle bone. First we thought it was just a sprain, but when it remained painful Norm put a cast on it. After a few days he heeded my pleas and gave me a walking cast. Then I could hobble to class on crutches. The cast turned out to be quite advantageous. The children were just learning to write their names. When one could write his or hers to my satisfaction, the child could write it on my cast.

Our most memorable letter that year turned out to be "Y." The Laubach-inspired reader had a picture for every letter. The word *yuyu* was excellent for "Y"; it means "spider." The book had a picture of a spider in a spider web, with a few lines darkened to make the "y." We did better, through no initiative of mine. It never occurred to me until just now to thank God for it, but I suppose he must have sent that nice large garden spider to the back wall of our unpainted concrete classroom. I gratefully marched to the back of the room with my chalk and wrote *yuyu* under the spider. I wonder if my children remember that as well as I do?

Then of course we had arithmetic. They brought in bottle caps or sticks for counting and seeing addition and subtraction facts. And the curriculum included practical education, like sewing on buttons. The youngest little girl sewed her first button from the center holes to the edge all around. Of course, then you can't put it through the buttonhole.

And there was Show and Tell. We went to see some things, and the children were encouraged to bring in objects. They had to be taught to ask questions. One girl brought in the framework of an umbrella. Classmate's question: "Where did you get it?"

My question: "What do you suppose an umbrella is made of?"

One girl's delightful suggestion: "Bat wings?"

Another advantage my class had—there were only 20 pupils. There were 21 the first day, but one little boy died that afternoon. The second day we went to his funeral. He had been so weakened by repeated malaria that his little body couldn't take a worm cure.

Thank God there were no more fatalities during the year. One charming little boy fell into an outhouse hole (outhouses in Congo have no seats), but he was pulled out, disgusting but safe.

Classes in the regular schools would start out with 50 or 60 children. Then when the first exam time came, those who had not been able to pay their school fees (although their parents had bought those notebooks) were weeded out. The oldest boy in my class was ten. He had started school several times but never been able to pay the fees. It was a big help to have such a mature and knowledgeable child in the class.

In the latter part of the school year we studied the story of Joseph (omitting Potiphar's wife). These children had the advantage that there were books in their small homes, including the Bible. As they advanced in reading, occasionally one would slip in beside me in church and read the Bible along with me. They learned the sounds of all the letters in first grade, but consonant blends (two consonants together) didn't come till second grade. That meant I had to limit the vocabulary. I couldn't use the very common word *yandi*, which means "he" or "she." (If we had it in English it would make gender inclusiveness so much simpler!) When I wrote the daily episode of Joseph on my chart I had to repeat Yosefi every time. We enjoyed the story of Joseph, and I decided to try creative drama, the children figuring out how to act out the various scenes. I thought it went well, except that, since the Joseph story includes so many men and almost no women, some male roles had to be played by girls; Jacob and Joseph were not willing to embrace when they met in Egypt. Well, Joy suggested we enact the play for the parents. Since the geography of the story is so wide ranging, I had the bright idea of having the children perform on tables placed around the perimeter of the room, with the audience in the middle. Guess what. Only the people on the outside chairs could see the action. I guess you probably figured that out without having to see it demonstrated. Also, when we actually did the play in practice, it fell completely flat. I was ready to scrap it, but Joy suggested I narrate it as the children played it, and that worked pretty well.

At Christmas time I gave each child a present—a piece of paper with a story typed on it that they could read. Remember, they had no book; up till now they had read only from the blackboard, the easel, and their slates. Now they had a story they could hold in their hands, take home with them, read to their parents.

The curriculum also called for a little French. The children learned to answer *"Qu'est-ce que c'est?"* (What is it?) with the names of common classroom objects. From there we started a little very basic conversation. Occasionally they were also exposed to a little poem or song in French. One of them was *"Escargot,"* about a snail. The children knew what snails were. We didn't discuss eating them. One day one little girl begged, "Let's do *Escargot*. Let's not do *Qu'est-ce que c'est.*"

Came the close of the school year and exam time. For their reading test, I wrote an exercise on each child's slate—a slightly different one for each child, so there was no temptation to peek at someone else's work.

Everybody passed! One little boy made just 50 in every subject—and I didn't cheat. Now 50 is passing in the Congo, as in France and Belgium. This fellow's mother was the weakest student among the wives, and his dad had been moved from the upper level to the lower, so I guess heredity was showing up. He did make 50. The little boy who could not learn the letter "K" still read *"me"* for *"ke,"* but otherwise he did all right. Some were reading their daddies' Bibles!

After graduating to public health work—the exciting job of developing a new Rural Health Zone, training nurses to run Health Centers, not just dispensaries, and recruiting mature, knowledgeable women to oversee health concerns in the villages—after ten years of that, Norm was back in general medical practice, assisting the Congolese doctor at Kikongo with patient care, and also doing some informal training of nurses and auxiliaries, at the hospital and at the rural health centers which Dr. Kwata had

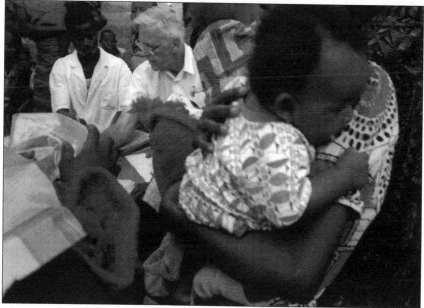

Well baby clinic

established. Norm had worked under a Congolese hospital administrator at Kimpese and under another missionary doctor at Vanga, but this was his first time to work under a Congolese doctor. It was easy, because Norm respected him and they worked together well, each appreciating the other's strengths. The doctors were pleased to see results of their baby vaccination program—only a few scattered cases of measles, rather than the yearly epidemic that had usually occurred. After nine months at Kikongo Norm saw the first case of newborn tetanus. That baby had been born at a nearby Catholic mission and had not been vaccinated. Kikongo hospital quickly invited that mission to come receive supplies of vaccine. What a change from the early days, when Catholics and Protestants were at each other's throats, each thinking the other's converts were lost forever!

Norm appreciated contact with patients—praying for them, encouraging them, helping them forgive their relatives and be forgiven. Some Congolese were surprised and gratified that he, a white man, understood that need. He found opportunities too to share Christ, and a deeper understanding of Christ, with members of the hospital staff.

Tuberculosis, a disease of malnutrition, was rampant. With modern TB medicines, Norm was able to send patients back to their villages where food was available, the health center nurse giving daily injections and follow-up. The next step was to train the rural nurses to diagnose TB and start treatment promptly, sending complicated cases to the hospital. In 1986, at age 60, Norm wrote, "We have just sent out three nurses with whom I spent two or three hours a day over a two-month period retraining them for rural health work. This has given me new ideas." He and Dr. Kwata were to give an intensive three-week course—including 120 class hours and practical training in community health work—to ten nurses, over half of them from the old government medical service.

Our second year at Kikongo I went from first grade to the pastors' school! I was asked to teach psychology and pedagogy. In college I had taken only one beginning class in psychology, but I was given a good textbook and I chose topics that were relevant to my students. The different kinds of freedom, or liberty, for instance. There's personal freedom—you're not a slave; civil freedom—you're not in prison; national freedom—your country is independent. It was good for them to make a distinction. Another topic was lying. What is lying, and what isn't?

Figurative language—the use of metaphor—is not lying. When Song of Solomon says, "Your lips are a red ribbon," it's not meant to be taken literally. If I say something untrue but I think it's true, that's a mistake, not a lie. African fables in which animals talk and cook are not lies; they're not meant to be taken literally. A lie is intended to deceive. When you lie to your toddler, what are you teaching him? Mama is far away, working in her garden. You're home with the kid, he's crying, and you say, "Stop crying, or that goat out there will eat you."

Maybe the kid believes you and stops. But someday he's going to realize that goats don't eat children, and he will have learned not to trust Daddy.

"Well, what are we to do when the child cries?"

"Why is he crying?"

"He's hungry."

"Give him something to eat."

"Nothing in the house."

"Then when you get your rations, be sure there are some bananas he can eat when he's hungry."

That may not sound like a psychology course, but it's what seemed useful to me.

I figured pastors would probably need pedagogy primarily for teaching Sunday School. I suggested that when they taught the creation story to children who had heard it for several years before, they have a new objective, perhaps to show that God wanted good for his people. I asked, "Don't some of your parishioners think of God as an angry man in the sky waiting to punish them when they do wrong?"

One student answered, "Why, yes, that's what we all believe."

Really?! I don't believe they all did, but at least he did.

I don't believe they all did, because the Scripture Union was very strong. One missionary colleague called it the cutting edge of Christianity in the Congo at that time. The Holy Spirit was working. Scripture Union members were concerned about evangelism, discipling, and prayer. One man told Norm, "I felt I needed preparation for this work, so I've spent the last 24 hours fasting and praying."

One day in class one of the students expressed a concern. Speaking of another student, he said, "When we joyfully raise our hands in prayer, he doesn't. Do you suppose he has a demon?"

I answered, "It seems to me the Holy Spirit gives us the freedom to raise our hands or not raise our hands." I thought but fortunately refrained from saying, "If a demon is involved, it seems more likely that he's influencing the one who criticizes his brother."

At Kikongo we enjoyed the help of two volunteers who became our first Catholic Baptists. One was a Peace Corps young woman who went back to Vermont both Christmases she was there, returning with real maple syrup each time. The other was a mature woman, a doctor from Cook County Hospital in Chicago. They both helped a great deal with the work, and both these Catholic women joined in the missionaries' Bible study.

That second year I was more involved with the dynamic women's group at Kikongo. In fact, I served as leader of one of the twelve groups into which the large fellowship was divided. We were using a book on James, designed for Theological Education by Extension. One day some women who could read were going over the lesson at my house before meeting in the large group. Included was our excellent hospital chaplain's wife, who served as a chaplain too. In one of the Bible verses printed in the book there was a misprint, a zero that did not belong there. This woman thought of it as an "O" and found two spiritual meanings for that misprint!

The women in Jean's small group

One day in the large group the women were discussing what to do when your child is sick and not improving with medical care. Animist family members are urging you to go to the sorcerer. (We used to say witch doctor.) It's a real problem. The lovely wife of the administrator of the pastors' school testified, "I'm so blessed I don't have that problem. All of our family on both sides are Christian."

That year it was decided that the Christmas pageant would be given by the women. "Mama Abell, you'll be Simeon."

"What will I do for a beard?"

"Make one from a coconut."

Norm had once taken a course in Addis Ababa, Ethiopia. He had brought back one of the large, thin, white cotton cloths Ethiopians use to keep off the sun and the flies. This made a fine prayer shawl. That church had choir benches on the platform perpendicular to the pews, so when we actors sat there waiting for our turn the congregation saw us in profile, and saw only the end person very well. When I stood up and went center stage, there was an audible gasp. Here was this man in prayer shawl and beard, with a white face! Is it a ghost? Then I started speaking. What a relief! It's just Mama Abell.

Marjorie and Rory were in France where Rory was completing his Master's. When he achieved that, they were able to spend a summer with us at Kikongo. Rory taught in the Pastor's school and Marjorie helped Norm at the hospital. She also found an opportunity to help one of the women with sewing. While they were there, this dear couple stayed in another missionary's house. The usual occupants had to leave for medical reasons. Here our daughter and her husband met an inconvenience we had never encountered. Oh, we had seen spiders, but this house was spider heaven! Rory remembers combatting the spider plague with a can of Baygon (insecticide) in one hand and a broom in the other. Fortunately this experience didn't keep Rory from subsequent visits to Africa. It was an unexpected delight to have them with us. It's wonderful that all of our children are grateful for their experiences in the Congo, both in growing up years and later visits. Marjorie says, "I wouldn't trade it for anything!"

Kikongo had been selected for a mission station partly because it boasted seven springs where people could get water and bathe. There could be one for men, one for women, one for schoolboys and one for girls—and three to spare! Norm, being a doctor and the son of a sanitary engineer, was interested in springs. One day he visited three of them, climbing down into the valley and back up again each time, since they were in different valleys. Then he made another trip down to the ram, which used water pressure to pump water up to our houses and the hospital. Back at home, his legs cramped excruciatingly. He'd had leg cramps from time to time ever since he had polio; he would stand up and the cramp would go away. This time there was no possibility of being able to stand. After some time I thought of filling the solar shower bag with hot water. The shower bag was meant to hang from a tree branch where the tropical sun would heat the water. It hadn't been solar heated that day, so I filled it with hot water from the stove. Norm was able to slide down from his chair so his legs were on the floor, and I put the heated bag between them. Gradually the cramps eased. That was the first indication we had of post-polio syndrome, although we didn't recognize it at the time. People who've had polio and recovered enough to live active lives often overuse the muscles they have left to make up for those that don't work any more. Then, 20 or 30 years later, post-polio will attack those weary muscles, gradually depriving the person of his strength. Some time after that episode at Kikongo, on our way back to Zaïre from the States, we spent the night in a hotel in downtown Zurich. In the morning we walked around to see some of Zurich before making our way back to the train station to return to the airport. After some walking, Norm's legs just gave out. He had to sit and rest a while before we could head for the station. That was the second indication.

CHAPTER TWENTY

Moanza Again

After two years at Kikongo, in 1987, we were asked to move to Moanza. This would be our fourth short stay at that beautiful church center. We'd spent the last year of our first term there, everyone rejoicing that now that small hospital had its own doctor. Norm had turned the work over to Frank, who stayed there barely a month before being evacuated after the army revolt following independence. We had returned to Moanza as soon as possible, Norm cutting his furlough short and the rest of the family following later. Norm hadn't been there a year when polio sent him back to the States. After our polio furlough we'd worked two years at Vanga, under another doctor, and then gone back to Moanza to replace the head nurse going to the States for further training, much as our friend Kimpiatu from Sona Bata had done. That was to be only a three-year term, Norm coming back after polio, so again we were at Moanza only one year.

Now again it was a case of further training. Our second year at Kikongo, Dr. Kwata was free to study Public Health in Kinshasa since Norm was there to supervise the hospital and the Rural Health Zone. In mid-1987 Dr. Kwata was back at Kikongo, but the doctor at Moanza had been chosen to attend that same Public Health School. So back we went.

As you saw, we loved Moanza, but we had never stayed there longer than a year. In a sense we'd had three honeymoons there. This time we were there two years, and the honeymoon ended.

Problems were apparent from our arrival. Norm was immediately handed a letter making accusations against someone who was leaving. It was obvious that tension and jealousy were rampant, not just between tribes but even between villages. There was quite a bit of epilepsy, and the number of people suffering from river blindness had increased. Poverty was more evident. The road to Moanza was in worse shape than before. Our average speed coming in on that road was 20 kilometers (12½ miles) per hour. No wonder commercial truck drivers did not vie with each other for the Moanza market. Moanza women produced quantities of peanuts, but where could they sell them?

In the face of such poverty, Moanza was third in the Congo Baptist Convention in giving. At the weekly women's meeting the offering ran around 90 zaïres, about two zaïres per woman. At Kikongo most of the women gave nothing at the weekly meeting. After the meeting the Moanza women would sing and dance their way to the hospital to give food to the patients from their own meager stocks. Once I asked the school principal's wife, "What do you do when someone comes to your door begging for food?" There were so many!

She replied simply, "If I have it, I give it." I tried that solution. A boy came to the door asking for tomato paste. I had a carton of the tiny cans. I gave him one. Another boy came. I gave him one. The word spread, and before the afternoon was over the carton was empty. Then the boys who had not received tomato paste overpowered the smaller ones and took theirs away. Obviously it wasn't going to be that simple for me.

People were praying. At Kikongo the Scripture Union had been strong. Here at Moanza there were four Scripture groups, for men, for women, boys, and girls. One of the hospital nurses spent part of his vacation joining in an evangelistic campaign. Another asked us to pray for him as he set out to vaccinate a thousand village children who were not yet protected against measles. People came individually for prayer and counsel.

An especially bright spot was getting to know the Congolese area pastor and his wife, Jacques and Rose. When we got there Rose was beginning a literacy class. Years later she was chosen to head up the literacy program for the whole Convention.

The first of those two years at Moanza we lived in the house at the top of the airstrip, because Jack and Trissie were on home assignment. Bob and Anelise lived in the other missionary house next door. The house Cliff and Joy had occupied so long before was now Jacques and Rose's.

While we were there our daughter Grace and her family came to visit. Grace and Michael now had four children: Monique, Daniel, Marjorie, and five-month-old Matthew. Grace had wanted her family to see the country she'd grown up in, but Michael hadn't been interested. Now Michael, a professor of behavioral and biological psychology, had an opportunity for some summer study at St. Andrews in Scotland (where golf originated). It made sense to combine that trip with a visit to Moanza. Michael decided to do it before Scotland. Plenty of culture shock either way.

Michael brought along materials to test Congolese children, materials that did not depend on language. There were various wooden shapes to be fitted into holes, blindfolded I believe. And there were other tests. Michael found differences between Congolese and American children. Americans tend to name things in their minds, at least, before doing anything with them. These children would deal with the object in question without bothering to name it. "What do you suppose makes the difference, Michael?"

"Well, there could be differences in brain development from the environment in which they learn and adapt from very early childhood into their school years."

Monique celebrated her seventh birthday at Moanza, as her mother had done. The difference was that Grace had been there a while and could talk with the Congolese girls who came to her party. Monique had to manage without a common language. She was fascinated by insects, so for a birthday present we gave her a rhinoceros beetle, a large and fearsome looking insect. She was delighted. She kept it in a glass jar on the little divider that separated one side of the living room from the dining room. She wanted to be sure no one swept it off onto the floor by mistake, so she made a sign warning people to be CAREFUL, BEETLE. Remember, Monique had just turned seven. The sign actually read CARFUL, BEDDLE.

Monique had a creative mind and decided to produce a play. Granted, we were in Africa, but the play involved Native Americans. She draped blankets over a corner of the fenced-in yard to create a tepee. Five-year-old Daniel was not interested but agreed to play the fearless hunter. Twice he went out with bow and arrow and shot the same log, which he dragged home, Monique prepared, and they ate. Afterwards Monique scrubbed the dishes with sand.

Marjorie was only two and did most of her traveling on Daddy's back. Some of the women, concerned, asked if she was crippled. No, it was just a lot quicker to pick her up and carry her.

Michael discovered a boy in the workmen's village who had never been able to use his legs. He just sat on the ground all the time, crawling and dragging his useless legs when he needed to move. But his parents could tell he was intelligent; if he heard a plane overhead he would draw it in the sand. Michael took the initiative to have a special chair built so the boy could sit in school. His sister agreed to carry him on her back. And the boy started first grade. Later I gave a sample lesson in that class, and that boy caught on better than any of the others. He excelled in school, and he must have felt some satisfaction in being able to read and learn with other children, but he never smiled.

From that visit on, Michael was determined to come back to Africa and do something to help those children. While continuing to teach at his college, he earned a Master of Public Health degree at the University of Michigan and eventually became an adjunct professor there.

During that Moanza term our son Jim came. He had graduated from LeTourneau College with various pilot's and mechanic's licenses and got some flying experience on Cape Cod and was hoping to take over our colleague Jack's aviation ministry when Jack retired. Now he had come to learn to fly Jack's Short Takeoff and Landing (STOL) plane and to do the flying and maintenance of that plane while Jack and Trissie would be on furlough. He occupied the guest house where we had lived our last month at Moanza in 1960. He hadn't, of course. He wasn't born till '63. Jim in French is Jacques. Pastor Jacques was pleased that our son had the same name as he.

There was another young American around, David, a Peace Corps volunteer working on water supply. He lived in a very simple house in the village at the top of the hill above us. He was a fine young man, and he and Jim enjoyed each other's company. David did not want to be called Davidi, so he used his middle name, Sabin, with the French pronunciation. We missionaries (and the young men) got together on Sunday evenings. We read a biography of Jonathan Goforth together, and then *The Great Mission Advance,* an account of a large number of Baptist missionaries who sailed together from the States to the Far East in 1835, some to Burma, some to Thailand, some to China. While discussing the book someone remarked how sad it was that just ten years later the Southern Baptists split off from the Northern ones. The Northerners felt that slave owners could not be appointed as missionaries; how could they relate to people of color as brothers when they owned people of color? But the Southerners felt it was a great loss to exclude all slave owners. They pointed out that some Southerners inherited slaves, when they themselves might be against slavery. So the split came. When Sabin heard about this, he was shocked. The son of a Southern Baptist minister, he had always believed that Southern Baptists were directly descended from John the Baptist.

Remember the junior high I had directed back in '65–'66, two whole classes? It was now part of a secondary school of ten classes. With all these students in residence, the beautiful church, built of local pink and purplish stone, had become too small. The plan was to extend it on both sides. So we all took part, all who were able, in going down to the stream and bringing up rocks. The women carried them in baskets on their heads. I'm afraid I brought up only a couple of rocks each time.

One day on my way to church I was appalled at the litter covering all the area in front of the church. Students would freely rip pages or parts of pages out of their notebooks to write letters on or whatever, and freely throw papers on the ground. In front of people's homes the wives would sweep, but no one took the responsibility for cleaning up in front of God's house. Nor was there any bin or other place to put the litter. Well, approaching the church I picked up as much as my two hands would hold. Then what to do with it? When we went forward for the offering, I deposited my trash in an empty one of the little wooden offering boxes, explaining to the usher holding another box for the offering, "I picked this up in front of God's house. There's no place to put it." But the choir was singing loudly and he had no idea what I said.

Well! Great indignation! Mama Abell had committed sacrilege! She had put trash in the offering! After the offering Pastor Jacques called me forward. "Mama Abell, you may not take communion."

Later we talked in his office. I explained, "The courtyard in front of God's house looked so terrible, covered with trash. I brought some in to protest. Then there was no place to put it. I didn't realize the empty wooden box was sacred." When I finally used the word "sorry," the pastor decided I could be forgiven. The next Sunday he explained my side of the story to the congregation, called me forward, had me kneel, and restored me to fellowship. It's nice that a missionary can be disciplined by her African pastor.

When Jim had been flying with Jack for six months, it was time for a six-month checkup with an MAF (Mission Aviation Fellowship) pilot. The pilot came, and he and Jim went up in Jack's plane. Jack's wife, Trissie, was flight following. After a while she could not make contact with the plane. Of course she didn't tell us about that until later. Another MAF pilot was at Moanza, and he and Jack took off in the MAF plane to head towards a village airstrip where Jim and the other pilot had been planning to land. Shortly after they were airborne, they heard the signal of an emergency locator transmitter (ELT)!

Here's what had happened. The flight had gone well until Jim was to land at a certain airstrip. The plane was a tail dragger—no nose wheel but a tail wheel. Jim had landed the two main wheels, but the tail wheel had not yet come down to the ground when a goat ran onto the strip in front of the plane. Jim slammed on the brakes. The goat escaped scot free, but the plane did a somersault and landed on its back. It is not good for a plane to land on its back.

The two pilots, hanging upside down from their seat belts, asked each other, "Are you all right?" They each had a scrape down the front of their leg. That was all. Great relief. They got out of the plane, removed the ELT (which had not been activated by the relatively slow forward deceleration before the plane flipped over and made a rapid "backward" deceleration), and turned it on. They prayed a prayer of thanksgiving, then got help from the local villagers to drag the upside-down plane to the side of the airstrip to make room for the other plane to land. About that time their rescuers arrived.

The plane was trucked to Kinshasa, where Jim spent the next 15 months repairing it. MAF let him use their hangar space, gave him valuable advice, and shared their maintenance expertise. Our colleagues Willard and Norma—Norma had given Jim his first haircut at Vanga all those years before—invited Jim to live with them in the city. Their own son, a little older, had also graduated from LeTourneau and was on his own. What a boon for Jim! Part of the time he lived at the hostel, where he had been a school kid, helping the hostel parents when he wasn't working at the hangar.

The plane flew again, and Jim flew it a little more, but he did not replace Jack while he and Trissie were on furlough. They were back from furlough before the plane's repairs had been completed. However, the MAF people in Kinshasa had been favorably impressed with Jim during those 15 months of working side by side. They needed a pilot right away in the northwest part of the Congo and asked if he would serve temporarily. Jim began receiving a little financial support from US churches and friends through MAF, which the organization supplemented with a small salary. He went up to the northern border and flew for MAF for a little over a year.

Back in the US he got a degree in Missiology from Fuller Theological Seminary to prepare himself for appointment by American Baptists, but the board was not willing to appoint a missionary for aviation work. We already had one missionary seconded to MAF, and a teaching doctor for Vanga was seen as the greater need. So Jim did not fly for American Baptists, but he was accepted as a career missionary with MAF and is still with them.

His time at Fuller was not wasted. Oh, he learned a lot from his creative profs. In one January term the students were told, "Pick one of the 200 languages spoken in Pasadena and see how much you can learn by contacting people on the street and saying, 'I want to learn your language.'" They were required to spend six weeks learning a language completely different from any that they already knew. Jim chose Armenian. He found that people had varied reactions when he learned to say in their language something like, "I am like a baby learning your language." But more important, he met Candace, an active American Baptist from Terre Haute, Indiana, a Fuller student working on her Master of Divinity and also a crackerjack secondary school math teacher. Shortly after our retirement Jim and Candy were married, to their delight and ours.

Now Moanza received a wonderful gift. While we were still at Kikongo, Moanza had invited a brand-new doctor to come work there, first taking a two-year residency at Vanga. Prime (Preem) came from a village about 40 miles from Moanza. Although he had lived in cities almost all his life, he had kept in touch with his extended family and now felt a strong call to work at Moanza. With a rocky start and some difficulties along the way, Prime did follow the program at Vanga, marry a physiotherapist, and become the proud father of twin girls. In 1989 he arrived at Moanza. He and Melanie were delightful people, deeply committed Christians, and dedicated medical workers. Norm and Prime enjoyed working together very much.

The year is 1989. School is out for what we would call summer vacation. In that part of the Congo it's dry season. The high school principal asks me, "Will you teach English next school year?"

"Yes, I'll be glad to."

Then Norm is called back to Kikongo. They're starting a little school for auxiliary nurses, and he's needed. "Sorry, Mr. Principal, I won't be teaching here after all." He was not happy.

CHAPTER TWENTY-ONE

The Last Year

Back to Kikongo. Back to our good little house and our Kikongo friends. We don't know whether Purpose was happy or not. Oh, you don't know Purpose. When we lived at Kikongo before, we had been given a silver tabby kitten. She did not appreciate moving to Moanza. She did a lot of meowing, and we made several unnecessary stops along the way, trying to understand her needs. Norm stopped halfway to talk with the nurse at a Health Center. Purpose was glad to get out and stretch her legs. When we were ready to continue our journey, Purpose was nowhere to be found. We called. No kitty. We looked all around the vehicle and underneath it. No cat to be seen. Finally someone discovered her. She had found some projection under the car that she could lie on. We hadn't seen her on the ground; she was a little higher. OK, cat, back to purgatory. When we opened the car door at Moanza she immediately fled to Jack and Trissie's roof. She didn't come down for some time. Jack thought he could bring her down with a broom. That just intensified her desire to remain inaccessible. Eventually she did descend and decided to make Moanza her home. Why Purpose?

Because she purred more than any other puss I had known. When she reached the age of six months she produced her first litter, asking me to hold her paw (figuratively) for that first experience of labor. Only one kitten survived from that first litter. It was so soft I named it Whisper, and every subsequent kitten received a name that had either "per" or "puss" in it. All those Moanza kittens were silver tabbies like Mama. Now at Kikongo she had a new mate and produced black and white kittens. One had a black circle about the size of a penny on the back of its neck, so it was named Per Cent. Another got stepped on but managed to survive; we named it Perseverance. We gave one kitten to the chaplain's wife, who named it Nkundi, which means "friend." That was unusual; Congolese don't ordinarily think of animals as friends.

Norm's principal job this year was directing (and teaching in) the new nursing school. Mr. Nsiny, the head nurse, also taught. A lovely female nurse named Itey (ee-tay-ee) had been working at Kikongo since she graduated from the Vanga nursing school in 1987. Now she supervised

Nurse Itey and two of her students

the students' work on the wards and in the Rural Health Centers. She also taught nursing technique in the classroom and supervised the girls' dorms. Busy lady. We had 17 students that first year.

I taught a class that I suppose was called *séminaire*. One boy was a Jehovah's Witness. I asked him what differences he saw between their way of doing things and ours. The only difference he could think of was that Jehovah's Witnesses celebrate communion only once a year!

Another day we talked about AIDS, called SIDA in French. Young people in particular liked to pooh-pooh the existence of AIDS, calling it *Syndrome Imaginaire pour Décourager les Amants* (Imaginary Syndrome to Discourage Lovers). I asked them, "Have any of you seen someone die of AIDS?"

One girl had lived in Kinshasa and replied sadly, "I have." No one mentioned "Imaginary Syndrome" in my presence again. Norm saw his first case of AIDS at that hospital. We had previously heard about a man on the staff at IME who had died of AIDS. He had been a generous blood donor. How many others had he infected?!

One of the students developed rheumatoid arthritis and had to be assigned easy tasks like dealing with linens instead of the regular ward work the others had to do. All the students passed at the end of the year, and a new first-year class of 15 was added. We stayed for the first months of that second year, departing at the end of October.

It was hard to leave all the work in the hands of Dr. Kwata, Mr. Nsiny, and Miss Itey. We had hoped to be there until another doctor arrived. We weren't able to do that, but there was one on the way.

Doctors at IME recommended Dr. Ibi. Medical students in Kinshasa have only classroom work at the medical school; their last year they are farmed out to various hospitals. You read about that when we were at IME. Dr. Ibi had done that last year at IME and become known for his Christian character as well as his medical ability. His home was in the Bandundu Region but not very close to Kikongo. Would he be willing to work at this new place? Yes, he would! He answered Norm's letter enthusiastically and humbly. (Not all new doctors are humble!) He came to Kikongo for a visit, stayed with the Kwata family, and bonded with them almost immediately. When we left in October of 1990, he was in Kinshasa patiently pushing his assignment to Kikongo through the various government offices.

Remember our son-in-law Michael's visit to Moanza? His determination to return to Africa to help? Now he had learned of a Fulbright grant to enable an anthropologist or an economist to do research in Africa for a school year. Michael, of course, was a behavioral and developmental psychologist, but he applied anyway, did a great deal of work making the necessary contacts and getting the necessary recommendations—and was awarded the grant. He came with the family to Kikongo shortly before school started in 1990 and stayed till the summer of 1991. He enlisted several Congolese helpers and tested school children at our church center and also at a Catholic mission, checking, among other things, what difference medical treatment (against worms, malaria, and the like) made in their cognitive ability and educational performance. When the year was over he recorded his and his family's experience in a delightful and impressive book entitled *The Accidental Anthropologist*. And he continued his interest in Africa and ways to help.

Michael was now under the umbrella of the US State Department at the embassy in Kinshasa (which administered the Fulbright program in Zaire) and eligible to patronize the US commissariat. When the rest of the family boarded an MAF plane for Kikongo, he stayed in Kinshasa for a few days, following up with the people he had enlisted to support his project and doing various errands. That first evening at Kikongo, Grace, Monique, Daniel, Marjorie, and little Matthew were gathered around the dining room table with us when flying ants decided to swarm. They came out from between the bricks of the walls and flew around. The children were naturally frightened. Monique

Uncle Jim brings goodies for Grace and Michael's children

particularly ducked whenever an ant flew by. Much later I reminded her, "Remember how scared you were of the flying ants your very first evening at Kikongo?"

And she confessed, "Oh, I was scared at first, but then I enjoyed dramatizing it."

Daniel had a birthday, with presents to unwrap. One looked especially inviting, a toy car. His dad exclaimed, "You're going to be the envy of all the Congolese boys." Alas! As he opened it we remembered that we had packed medicines in that empty box. Daniel's focus that year was soccer. If he wasn't playing soccer with other boys, he was standing on the sidelines watching the men play.

Marjorie found a playmate in the missionary girl next door. Their favorite activity was running down the slope in front of our house. The joys of a simple life! Three of our grandchildren joined the children's choir Mama Thérèse was leading. They sang well in French! They may even have understood what they were singing.

Dr. Grandpa and Grandma taking care of little Matthew

Norm had gone back to the States in January to be with his sister, who was dying of cancer. When he returned he brought a camcorder. I took some videos of him and of the other medical personnel. When we returned to the States we left the camcorder with Michael, who made very good use of it. Eventually Norm looked at a video of himself teaching and remarked in some surprise, "In January I was able to reach the top of the blackboard!" In the meantime post-polio had been taking its toll.

We came to the last week. The local people put on a feast in our honor in the largest classroom, with lots of food and speeches. Then the last Sunday. Formal farewells in church. At the end people followed us home and sang and sang in front of our little house. Finally we clapped our hands in appreciation and went inside. I wonder whether there was something else we should have done.

We left household stuff with Grace. When that family returned to the States they would give it away. We made boxes for a few special pieces, like my portable Irish harp and a chief's chair that came apart as two pieces of wood.

And then our 34 years in the Congo were over. Our other three children and their children were in the States. Our Congolese friends we would never see again. We would keep in touch by mail for a while. We left each other in God's hands.

CHAPTER TWENTY-TWO

If We Had It To Do Over

We would listen. Listen more and talk less. Ask more questions. Find out where other people are coming from before we judge. Try not to judge! If other people aren't doing what we want, it may be they don't understand us. Try to understand them.

Michael understood so much in the short year he was in Zaïre, some things we had never learned in all our years. And he did it without knowing much of the language. Of course he's a psychologist, but no doubt we could have tried harder.

I remember trying to teach religion to a second-year nursing class at IME. I was very discouraged with that class. They did not seem to care about the patients they should have been learning to serve. And I tried to change them by scolding and punishing. If I could do it over, I would throw away the textbook I was trying to follow and devote all my efforts and prayers to helping them realize God loved them. Surely that's the prerequisite for extending love to others.

Once the national soccer team, the *Léopards,* won the Africa Cup. The President declared a national holiday. At the time I regretted one

255

more day lost to teaching, but now I have a better appreciation for what a feat that must have been.

One thing we never understood until we read about it after we retired. We would occasionally invite Congolese over for a meal and were disappointed that they never invited us. When Norm was back at Moanza for five months without the family, he invited himself to Congolese homes, taking along a can of corned beef to make his visit less of a burden. That was certainly not in the culture. The article we read pointed out that Congolese hospitality is different. If anyone comes to a Congolese home for any reason, he is always offered at least a soft drink. If he comes at mealtime, he's invited to share the meal. If someone came to our house at mealtime, I would say, "We're eating now. Could you come back later?" How gross! How impolite! And I never realized.

This should have clued me in. One day at Vanga I was feeling frustrated and just started walking on a path, not knowing where I was

Remembering

256

going. Eventually I came to a little village, at least a cluster of houses. A woman came to a door, greeted me, and brought out two chairs for us to sit on, and we talked a little. After a while I went home, refreshed. The next day the woman showed up at our house at Vanga, bearing a chicken! She hadn't been able to show me hospitality when I was there so now she was making up for it.

There's a verse in Psalm 37 that says, "Don't give in to worry or anger; it only leads to trouble." Knowing that is one thing; doing it is another. If we could do it over again, we would plead with the Father, or the Holy Spirit, to deliver us from anger, which spoiled our witness so many times, and to give us understanding and wisdom as we talked with people. No matter how hot it was, how tired we were, or if we had malaria, speaking in anger was never the right response.

One thing we did do right was inviting people over to pray. We did it only once or twice at Vanga, regularly one year at Moanza, once in Kinshasa. We would do it much more. And I would remember that women like to pray with other women, men with men.

I would make sure to write our parents every week. I started out that way, but there were (many) times when I neglected that pleasant duty. When we talked with other members of their retirement community, we would hear how Dad went to the post office every single day and Mother never failed to ask, "Is there a letter from Jean?"

At least 11 days out of 12 Dad had to reply, "No, dear, not today."

I would also try much harder to write to our supporters regularly. That was one thing that too often got neglected. But I found time to read fiction. Our missionary children, and present missionaries with our board, are required to communicate regularly with their network of support. We were requested to.

We would also pray more in our home. We always planned to have daily devotions with our children but somehow it never became a regular practice. Our kids remember reading books together on the veranda at Sona Bata in the evening, and it was good, but we should have been reading the Bible too, and other books that would help us grow spiritually.

And I would pay more attention to our children. Back before we ever left the States, a neighbor had remarked, "She forgets she has children." She was right! When Grace found her daddy with the whole surgical team kneeling around a patient on our living room floor; when the man with a gun came through my bedroom window and I yelled at the top of my voice; and when we left a teenager in the city and got absorbed in our work down-country—I forgot I had children. When they didn't write I assumed they were all right. It wasn't until after our retirement, when Grace shared a book called *Letters Never Sent*, that I began to realize how different the adjustment is for missionaries' children—third culture kids—than for missionaries.

How good God is! He guided our children's growth, with the help of other Christians, and molded each one into such a great person, in spite of our neglect. Thank you, Father.

In any of these areas, we can't go back and do it over, can we? In the days when we showed slides to church groups, we liked to close with a picture taken inside the little church at Songololo, one of several churches built by our colleague Elmer. In the wall behind the platform is a lighted cross. We would ask people, "Where does the light come from?" It was not electricity. The wall was made of concrete blocks, and holes had been pierced in the blocks that formed the cross. The light was sunlight. We could say, "We went to the Congo to pierce holes in walls so the light of God's love could shine through." Did we do that? Sometimes. Sometimes not. We thank God for the times we did listen to his wisdom and his will, and for bringing good even out of our mistakes. And I think of the names of some of our Congo friends, and the faces of others, many gone on now—it's been 29 years since we said those good-bys at Kikongo— and pray his blessing on them and their children and grandchildren, and on that country, now called the Congo again, with all its problems and promise, and every person in it loved and cherished by the Father.

Made in the USA
Middletown, DE
29 December 2019

82104494R00161